Chapter One

THE WORK OF THE HONEYBEE

Before we delve into the bounty of folklore inspired by bees and beekeeping, it is useful to understand the functionality of a hive, the role of the beekeeper and the work of the honey-bearing bee (*Apis mellifera*).

There are three members in a working hive: the queen, the worker bees (female) and the drones (male). The queen has the capacity to lay up to two thousand fertilised eggs a day. Without the queen, a hive would simply not survive. She is at the heart of the bee colony and is responsible for pumping life into the hive. By secreting a pheromone, which is carried throughout the colony by her dutiful worker bees, the queen dictates the movements, behaviours and social order of her kingdom. When introducing a new queen to a hive, Dad would transport her in a Cara matchbox. He would mark her back with a dot of red nail varnish to ensure she was easily found after she had been wholly accepted into the hive. To heighten those odds, he would gently insert the matchbox between two combs, leaving it slightly ajar. The bees would eat through the cardboard and eventually free the queen who, over time, adapted to her new surroundings by absorbing its smell and so be welcomed by the colony as one of their own.

Queens are recognisable by being slightly longer and plumper than worker bees. Worker bees are the smallest in physical size, which enhances their ability to leave the hive, gather pollen and be productive. Drones are heavier and stockier in appearance, but typically are not as long as the queen bee. In a crowded hive, the location of the queen is easily determined by the overcrowding caused by worker bees competing to attend to her. The worker bees feed, preen and clean their queen.

Bee colonies are completely matriarchal in their organisation and framework. Female worker bees have multiple roles and responsibilities in the hive. In addition to being servants to their queen, they regulate the temperature of the hive by the movement of their wings, renovate comb cells and guard the colony against foreign intruders. Their ability to sting heightens their effectiveness in this regard. Once they sting, however, they pay the ultimate price. As a sting is barbed, it becomes embedded in the flesh of the adversary. When the bee tries to free herself, the stinging mechanism and nerve strands are left behind, causing her to die. However, her forfeited life will not have been in vain. The severed sting emits an odour, or an alarm pheromone, which can guide other bees to the target or act as a warning sign to stay away.

Importantly, worker bees are the pollen gatherers and foragers. It is their toil that ultimately results in the production of honey. Although they are the smallest in stature, the female workforce is responsible for ensuring that this society thrives.

Other than contributing to temperature control, the drone's sole function is that of reproduction. Drones rarely leave the hive, which, in terms of evolution, may account for them never having developed a sting, as they have never needed to protect themselves. Their contribution to the colony does not merit their survival all year round. Come autumn, once their purpose of impregnating the queen is complete, they are an unnecessary burden on the hive. Drones are fed by the workers and, being larger in size, their maintenance is a drain on resources and an unwelcome pressure on space. When mating season has passed, the drones are ousted from the hive by the worker bees, who, in addition to being the nurses, guards, grocers, housekeepers and construction workers, also take on the role of undertaker.

In folklore, this act of killing is described as 'the massacre of the drones': the worker bees sting the males and eject them from the hive. Although a small portion of worker bees will die as a result, this loss will not affect the overall health of the hive, as drones account for approximately fifteen per cent of the hive's population. Some drones will be injured rather than killed and, once ousted from the hive, they will be forbidden re-entry by the guard bees on patrol. The killing and expelling of the drones contribute to good housekeeping ahead of the winter months. Often, worker bees are seen working in pairs, dragging the dead carcasses of slain drones outside the hive. What remains is an efficiently run matriarchal society composed of the queen and worker bees.

Throughout winter, a beekeeper will often supplement the food available to bees by feeding the colony a syrup of sugar and water. Naturally, a bee would be able to survive on its own honey stores during the winter should they not be fully harvested by the keeper. Many beekeepers, however, take all the honey stocks from the hive and substitute it with syrup. Old stories depict this food substitute taking different forms, from brown sugar to new milk, with mentions of porter and ale on occasion! There are descriptions in folklore of bees enjoying ale and the guards dragging drunk bees back into the hive. A more surprising foodstuff is the tradition of roasting a small bird on a fire and placing it at the entrance of the hive. Larger birds – roasted fat hens, in fact – are also suggested as good winter feed.

Alongside consistent and regular feeding, another key factor that influences the health and productivity of a hive is its location. In the Irish climate, it is hardly surprising that apiaries, or collections of beehives, are mostly found nestled in sheltered areas, with one side of the hive facing a hedgerow. Location is a vital decision: choosing an area that is bountiful with flowers and vegetation will affect the nectar collected and impact the flavour and consistency of honey produced. Beekeepers can use this to their advantage and manipulate their own unique taste by purposely planting specific crops around their hives or by finding a sweet spot that naturally provides a perfect blend. Dad has been fortunate to be able to keep hives in a number of places in Dublin, including Kilgobbin, Stepaside and Airfield Estate (formerly known as Airfield Trust) in Dundrum, with different flavours of honey resulting from each location.

Positioning a hive with a southerly aspect, combined with it being surrounded by trees and flourishing plains, has long been cited as vital for the quality of honey harvested. Heathery hills are seen as particularly favourable in old accounts of the dos and don'ts of beekeeping. In folklore, it is said that the bees can detect heather-laden areas specifically, knowing that heather creates particularly flavoursome honey.

One activity that is quite out of the control of a keeper is the act of swarming, which is when a cluster of bees leaves the hive and settles or alights elsewhere, such as the branch of a tree or the eaves of a house. The two main reasons that trigger swarming are overcrowding and the birth of a new queen. Either incident causes a portion of the bees to rise and leave the hive. One beekeeper's loss can be another keeper's gain, if one is willing and able to catch a swarm and rehome the bees quickly.

Methods of collecting swarms can vary, but rules of thumb apply. Depending on the location of a swarm, the cluster can generally be shaken into a temporary enclosure, be it a skep (a straw hive) or a cardboard box. One vigorous shake to the football-like structure is ideal to ensure the cluster remains in one unit. A bedsheet is useful, as it can be wrapped around the swarm, confining the bees and shading them from sunlight.

As a teenager, I would often accompany Dad when he travelled across Dublin to collect swarms. We would regularly get phone calls from panicked households asking for an unwanted swarm to be removed from a house or garden, particularly on hot summer days. It was perceived by the caller as an amazing service, and by Dad as an opportunity to access a new hive of bees: a win-win!

Dad and I would wait until evening before attempting to collect and rehouse a swarm. At dusk, bees will be calmer and more sedate, having full bellies after a day of foraging nectar. However, bees in a swarm will be more agitated as they are exposed to the elements and feel less protected as a result. A swarm will always alight with the queen in tow, alongside approximately a third of the worker bees. In a tightly clustered swarm, the bees work together to shelter their queen and can be territorial, being in fear of her safety. It is hardly surprising that these contributory factors will make the bees more agitated and prone to stinging at this time.

When I was stung, which was often, Dad removed the sting with the poison sac as quickly as possible to prevent the spread of the venom. I remember placing Reckitt's Bag Blue on the wound to alleviate the swelling. Blue bags were used to whiten laundry and their primary ingredient was baking soda. Traditionally, baking or bicarbonate soda was the most commonly documented remedy for the alleviation of inflammation caused by a bee sting. The juice of an onion was also a popular cure, as was clay, bruised plantain leaves and cod liver oil. An alternative method of removing a sting involved the use of a key. Accounts from Carlow, Waterford and Kildare recommend teasing out the sting using the barrel of an old-fashioned watch key. An account collected in County Cork specified that the key of a door should be used. Presumably, one of the curative values of keys derived from the coldness of the metal on the skin.

When it comes to protection from bee stings, Dad has always been a minimalist in terms of his beekeeping costume. In the early days, he had a straw hat, with some hand-stitched netting along the brim. The netting would meet his shoulders and, other than that, his smoker was his only ally. Dad made his own smoker, with leather bellows and a metal cylinder. To light it, he would use a piece of cloth combined with long grass and rushes. I loved the smell of the smoker as a child. I recall Dad explaining why smoke pacified the bees: they associate smoke with their forest being on fire and it prompts them to cluster together for protection. This lessens their wing movement and heightens their chances of surviving the fire. This reaction has ancient evolutionary origins and today the smoker affords that same warning signal to huddle up, stay calm and weather the elements.

Before the introduction of a modern-day beekeeper's suit, usually involving white overalls zipped to a semicircular headpiece, people used more basic raw materials such as bonnets of hay. Dad maintains that whenever he wears his corduroy trousers while beekeeping, he tends to get stung more frequently because the bees mistake the corduroy for the fur of an animal. For this reason, he has opted for the more orthodox beekeeping suit in recent times.

It is not coincidental that beekeepers' outfits are generally white in colour. Experiments have proven that bees see colour. The photoreceptors in their eyes make them sensitive to the blue, green and ultraviolet light spectrum and they are blind to the colour red. White is considered to induce a calmness in bees and blue is said to instigate a sense of serenity. To encourage tranquillity, beehives were commonly painted blue, and in Britain this practice was also believed to guarantee a stronger honey yield. In Ireland, beekeepers often planted bluebells around their hives, as it was believed that the flowers would encourage the bees to work harder. To ensure this productivity, children were discouraged from removing the bluebells and were warned that, if they picked the blue flower during the day, a dead man would come for them that night. In County Carlow, this is why bluebells, or wild hyacinths, were known as 'dead man's fingers'.

Harvesting the honey is the beekeeper's reward and takes place at the end of the bees' working season in early autumn. In rural Ireland, the extraction of honey coincided with the potato harvest. Like any crop, factors – primarily weather related – will affect the quality and quantity of honey produced. My father estimates that he collects up to 80 or 90 lb (35 or 40 kg) of honey from one hive after a good season.

To remove the honey from the comb, an extractor is commonly used by beekeepers. This a large metal cylinder that allows approximately four to six combs to be attached vertically. Either manually spun, or via a push of a button, the combs rotate; centrifugal force draws the honey from the comb and splashes it onto the walls of the extractor. The honey, or liquid gold as Dad refers to it, can then be poured into jars via a tap at the end of the barrel.

Before extractors were commonly available in Ireland, people removed honey from the combs manually. This was a slow and arduous process, as each honey cell had to be pricked with a needle and the honey squeezed by hand into an earthenware pan. Impurities that rose to the top, such as bits of broken comb or grubs, were gently scraped away with a sharp edge. As honey contains antiseptic qualities, it can be stored nearly indefinitely without spoiling.

Come late autumn, when the weather gets colder and flowers stop growing, the bees retire into the hive and prepare for a leaner few months. The dispensable drones are ousted and the worker bees nestle in around their queen. And so the beekeeping season comes to a close for another year.

Chapter Two

THE ARRIVAL OF THE HONEYBEE INTO IRELAND

The earliest evidence we have for bees is a 75-million-year-old fossilised bee, encased in amber. Analysis of DNA sequences and fossilised bee burrows in South America suggests bees may even have been here over 100 million years ago, in the early Cretaceous, before dinosaurs were wiped out in the mass extinction event. Earlier civilisations and our ancestors used folklore to explain how bees came into existence and, through a wealth of lore and legend, bees are described as sacred in nature. They were said to be a gift from the gods, being all-knowing purveyors of truth and wisdom, with countless tales connecting them to the otherworld. Unsurprisingly, the lore that portrays their origin into the world also has supernatural and magical associations.

There are three popular folkloric theories that tell how bees originated on earth. Firstly, they are seen as a perpetual miracle, being created within paradise itself. A second theory, recounted in a legend from Ancient Egypt, describes the sun god Ra's tears transforming into bees as they fell to the earth. And lastly, they were said to originate magically from the depths of an animal carcass. The latter was noted in Virgil's *The Georgics* (Book IV) and was found in lore and legend thereafter.

The belief that bees derive from paradise is a popular and recurring motif. In paradise, bees signify purity and are aptly depicted as being white in colour and pure in nature. Their transformation to a darker, brown hue is said to have been a direct result of Adam and Eve succumbing to temptation and tasting the forbidden fruit in the Garden of Eden. Belief in their purity is given credence in laws written in the early nineteenth century. In 1841, the *Ancient Laws and Institutes of Wales* referred to the necessity of integrating beeswax candles into mass ceremonies. The law describes bees being gifted to the universe directly from paradise due to the first sin of humankind. Beeswax, in the form of church candles, is used to symbolise Christ's flesh; honey, being a celestial secretion from paradise, is rendered a fitting food of the gods.

Bees appear in hieroglyphs and also in a relief found in the Ancient Egyptian Sun Temple at Abu Gorab, dating from around 2400 BC. In fact, this relief is the earliest representation of beekeeping in practice. It shows beekeepers collecting honey from a wall of horizontal hives and passing combs to assistants, who pour the honey into large vessels. In Egyptian mythology, we are introduced to the notion of bees originating from the tears of the sun god Ra, or Re, who was a revered ruler of the earth and sea. His right eye signified the sun, his left the moon, and when he opened both eyes, there was light. When Ra wept, the tears that flowed from his eyes transformed into bees as they fell to the earth.

Irish folk tradition similarly embraces the belief that bees were introduced to the world via the tears of deities, often when experiencing pain and torment. An account from County Mayo tells of bees being created when Jesus was crucified. Tears fell from the eyes of Christ as he was being nailed to the cross. As each tear descended, it miraculously transformed into a bee and took flight into the sky above. Other Irish legends describe bees being created from the wounds of Job. Folklore tells of Job's agonising death, and how his body was inflamed by lesions from head to toe. As soon as his soul departed his lifeless form, a little bee emerged from each individual sore. Traditionally, this is why people applied beeswax as a pain-easing salve to abrasions on the skin, a practice still carried out today.

The earliest reference to the ox-born bee dates from 250 BC in the writings of Antigonos of Karystos. He presents the notion of bees taking form within the belly of animal carcasses, specifically in the ribcages of lions, bulls and oxen. The sheltered depths of an animal's carcass, it seemed, were the perfect cavity for bees to procreate. Varro, one of Ancient Rome's greatest scholars, wrote in the last century BC that rotten oxen are a perfect environment to create what he describes as 'the sweet bees, mothers of honey', a perception shared by Pliny the Elder, author of *Natural History*, which was published in AD 77–79. Varro also influenced Virgil, who described how the carcass of a bull calf is capable of spontaneously producing bees, which led to this hypothesis re-emerging within literature, poetry, lore and legend.

It is interesting that bees have been associated with both the sacred and the profane, from the tears of gods to the carcasses of dead animals. Bees are described as evolving from dead matter, from bones, which could be interpreted as a form of reincarnation, where the soul of the animal manifests as a bee. A magical tale, one that recurs in both Irish and international folk tradition, describes the souls of the departed leaving the body – of both humans and animals – in the form of a bee. When the last breath is drawn, a bee escapes the body through the mouth of the deceased, and bees are thus depicted as embodying the souls of the dead.

The association between the origin of bees and the carcass of an animal may come from the idea that a ribcage is a suitable enclosure within which a colony can build its comb and make its home. The ribs, being equal distance apart, could provide the perfect framework for bees to erect their comb uniformly. This image of bees nestling within an

The association between the origin of bees and the carcass of an animal may come from the idea that a ribcage is a suitable enclosure within which a colony can build its comb and make its home.

animal's ribcage is described in the adventure of Samson in the Book of Judges, when he observes a scout bee directing a swarm into a lion's carcass. Samson marvels at how nature, in the form of a ribcage, provides the perfect environment for bees to build their honeycomb and make their home.

As bees' origin on earth is largely described as mystical or divine in nature, it is understandable how the story of bees' arrival into Ireland is also imbued with pious associations. There are scientific theories as to how bees migrated to Ireland, but the folktale describing how bees were brought from Britain to Ireland is a lovely one. We are introduced to a devout sixth-century monk, Modomnoc (or Modhomnoc) of Ossory, who travelled to Wales to study in a monastery that was governed by David (the bishop of Mynyw, who was canonised in the twelfth century and became the patron saint of Wales). Being a hefty lad and a diligent worker, Modomnoc's first role in the monastery was managing a small building project. He found himself criticising another monk's tardy workmanship, which triggered a physical fight, resulting in a blow to the head for poor Modomnoc. On reflection, the monk blamed himself for inciting the fight. Who was he to criticise another man's efforts? He was overcome with regret, and presented himself to David to confess his transgression. Modomnoc was then offered an alternative role, as head beekeeper of the monastery's apiary.

As the months and years passed, Modomnoc became gentler and calmer in disposition as a result of tending the beehives. A bond developed between the monk and his bees, and they became inseparable. Nearing old age, Modomnoc decided to return to his homeland of Ireland. Because he had to travel by boat, he was forced to leave his bees behind. As he left the monastery, the bees were seen following him overhead like a little dark cloud. The monk returned the bees to the monastery's apiary and embarked on his journey a second time. However, his bees followed him to the harbour a second, and then a third time. They refused to be left behind. Modomnoc conceded and, with

It comes as no wonder to me that folklore presents bees' origin as sacred, mystical and otherworldly: their masterful ability to make honey, erect honeycombs and live and operate in a highly functional matriarchy keeps us in perennial awe of bees.

David's blessing, he took 'full of his bell of bees' back to Ireland. On his departure, David bestowed on him a prayer, asking God to bless the ground onto which he and his beloved bees landed, and imploring that his bees would flourish in their new home.

Folk memory gives different locations as the point of arrival of bees into Ireland, including Balbriggan, Kilkenny and Wexford. Interestingly, residents of Ballynaslaney, County Wexford, celebrate 6 March as the feast day of Saint David, and have named a holy well in his honour near the village of Oylgate. This is a nice nod to the saint who blessed Modomnoc's bees on their first voyage to Ireland.

In keeping with this legend of Modomnoc's bees coming to Ireland in the sixth century, native Irish words associated with beekeeping emerged at this time, such as *beach* (bee), *mil* (honey) and *míodh* (mead). A century later, Irish bee laws, or *Bechbretha*, were written, providing guidelines in terms of the rightful ownership of swarms and the repercussions should a beehive be stolen or a passer-by be stung. The existence of a specific set of laws relating to bees and beekeeping underlines their importance as a facet of life in early medieval Ireland.

It comes as no wonder to me that folklore presents bees' origin as sacred, mystical and otherworldly: their masterful ability to make honey, erect honeycombs and live and operate in a highly functional matriarchy keeps us in perennial awe of bees. The respect we bestow on bees is a thread running through lore and legend, and there is a recurring motif of bees being associated with Irish saints. The legends all serve to elevate the bees as virtuous, perceptive and intelligent little creatures.

Chapter Three

THE DIVINITY OF THE HONEYBEE

As I researched the folklore of bees and beekeeping in Ireland, the theme of bees as a divine or spiritual entity emerged. It only substantiated what I felt I already knew. Veneration is not something we are taught or told; it is something we witness and experience. I saw it in my father's respectful humility in relation to his bees. He tended to them, but he was not their master. I can picture Dad patiently watching a bee crawl on the back of his large hand, with respect and curiosity in equal measure.

Folklore offers us a tantalising window into the beliefs, practices and reverence that beckon the humble bee to take a seat among the divine. We have only to look at the rich benefits we reap from the labour of the bee to begin to recognise its noble standing; produce that brings light, has medicinal properties and sweetens. Honey, the 'food of the gods', was the first natural sweetener to be discovered by humankind. It is the primary ingredient in mead, the 'nectar of the gods', the world's oldest alcoholic beverage. Beeswax provided one of the first essential sources of light, burning purely, unlike the inferior smoky fumes created by tallow candles. Moreover, beeswax candles were the preferred option for religious ceremonies, the wax being perceived as emblematic of Christ's flesh. It would appear that the veneration of bees by the earliest of civilisations was both earned and justified. The fruits of the bees' labour positively impacted many facets of life and worship. What is fascinating about bees is their place in the realm of the sacred.

Many religious beliefs and practices, throughout generations, continents and diverse cultural contexts, hold a special place for the bee. In Peru, the Incas offered honey as a sacrifice to the sun. Babylonians built their temples on grounds that were consecrated by honey. The Hindu Rigveda gives the honeybee pride of place, elucidated in Sanskrit writings between 2000 and 3000 BC. In Mohammedan teachings, the bee is described as the only creature to be addressed directly by the Lord. And in the Bible, there are over sixty references to bees in the Old and New Testaments, some of which have entered popular vernacular over time. God calls on Moses to lead the slaves out of Egypt and escort them to a better place, a place of abundance, fertility and prosperity: 'a land of milk and honey.'

Divinities such as Vishnu, Indra, Krishna and Kama (the Hindu god of love) in the Rigveda and Mellona (an Ancient Roman goddess of bees) are described as having special encounters with bees, often symbolising a lesson learnt or a teaching received. In the Irish tradition, the animal kingdom and the natural world are deeply intertwined with lore and legend pertaining to Irish saints and are a dominant feature in Irish folklore from the fifth century onwards. This era, often referred to as 'the age of the saints', stretched from the fifth to the eighth centuries. Hagiographers – biographers of saints – celebrated the lives and missionary journeys of saints and documented miracles they performed and folktales they inspired, which has led to an interesting blend of pagan and Christian beliefs and traditions. The dominant feature of this bond between saints and the natural world is a camaraderie, an understanding and a mutual respect, which serve to ward off evil spirits and protect the wider community.

In a tradition where so few female saints are suitably celebrated, it is wonderful that bees have been assigned their own saint or patroness, Saint Gobnait. This special relationship and affinity is further explored in the next chapter, but there are a myriad of Irish saints who have specific associations with bees. On occasion, they inherit characteristics of bees and often appeal to the divine nature of bees for their stewardship, wisdom and protection.

Saint Bega, also known as Saint Bees, is one such example. She is described as incredibly pious and virtuous, as well as the most strikingly beautiful woman in Ireland. Daughter of an Irish king, Bega was promised in marriage to the King of Norway. However, she had vowed herself to an order called the Spouse of Virgins from infancy. Inheriting the virtue of bees that 'do not give themselves to love, do not seek pleasure which weakens' – as described by Virgil in *The Georgics* (Book IV) – Saint Bega desired a solitary life, one dedicated to her faith alone.

Fearing for her safety and chastity from the threat of pillaging Vikings, Bega fled Ireland to escape attack as well as the curse of an arranged marriage. Symbolically, she is said to have thrown herself into the sea and onto a floating skiff, or straw hive, which landed on the Cumbrian coast in AD 850. This is where she built her convent and made her home. The saint was observed to have 'hastened from place to place like a bee laden with honey' while caring for the sick and the poor. Today, St Bees is the place name given to a picturesque village on the Cumbrian coast where her feast day is still celebrated on 7 November and where there are several churches in her name.

Saint Brigid, the most revered Irish saint after Saint Patrick, shared similar life experiences with Saint Bega. She too opted for a pious life, to remain a virgin and to dedicate her life to charity and chastity. Stories about Brigid describe the special affiliation between the saint and the animal kingdom. She had the capacity to tame wild boar, could instruct foxes to perform tricks and she owned a white cow that produced milk endlessly. Legend describes

Brigid's miracles were plentiful. Most notable was the use of her cloak, or 'brat', which expanded in size when strewn on the ground.

her keeping her own bees and brewing mead from their honey. Professor Séamus Ó Catháin, in his 1995 book *The Festival of Brigit,* likened her to a queen bee, where both females represent mythical goddesses.

Brigid's miracles were plentiful. Most notable was the use of her cloak, or '*brat*', which expanded in size when strewn on the ground. When she sought land from Dunlang mac Enda, the King of Leinster, on which to build a monastery, he refused, until she asked for as much land as her cloak could cover. He foolishly agreed and when she spread her cloak, it miraculously grew to cover many acres. Other miracles describe her curing blindness with the touch of her hand, causing the Irish Sea to disappear with a simple prayer, and converting vats of water into mead or honey wine. She performed this miracle to save the reputation of her host, who was appointed to the job of preparing mead for the King of Leinster but failed miserably. Saint Brigid arose and blessed empty vessels, which miraculously filled with mead. Her feast day is 1 February, which is also Imbolc, or Imbolg. It traditionally marked the beginning of lambing season and today is celebrated as the first day of spring. This is when Saint Brigid's crosses are made from rushes and positioned in rafters of houses and roofs of stables in order to bless and protect all within. In 2022, Brigid was rightfully awarded her own national holiday in Ireland, to coincide with her feast day.

Honey hunters or beekeepers have their own patron saint: Ambrose, born in Germany (AD 339), reared in Rome and remembered as Saint Ambrose of Milan. Ambrose's first encounter with bees occurred when he was an infant. His father went to his son's crib to find his baby lying amidst a swarm of bees. Bees enveloped his arms, his legs and his head. To everyone's astonishment, Ambrose was left unscathed. Not a bee harmed the infant's face or body. His parents interpreted this as a divine manifestation, believing it to be the foretelling of Ambrose's future eloquence of speech. It was prophesied that he would be 'honey-tongued' in speech and gifted at uniting opposing voices. In the fourth century, Saint Ambrose was unanimously elected the Bishop of Milan and was known as a man skilled in the art of persuasion, having a sweetness of language and a comforting presence.

The discovery of bees hovering around babies whilst in a cot or cradle is a common motif in lore and legend. This visitation usually symbolises a gift being bestowed by the bees on the newborn, often in the form of eloquent speech or a boon of wisdom. The latter is said to be true of philosophers, poets and playwrights such as Plato, Pindar, Sophocles and Virgil. In all cases, the bees are perceived as spiritual messengers from the heavens, bestowing the gift of wisdom on the young child.

In popular tradition, over the last hundred years or so, Irish folktales have depicted a special bond between bees and priests. Folklore describes a bee's ability to differentiate between a priest and a lay person and shows bees honouring a devout and keen faith. In terms of their connection with the clergy, bees are seen to work in their favour, to obey and defend them as well as demonstrating a sensibility and deep adoration for the Blessed Eucharist. Moreover, bees exhibit a fitting level of reverence for what is considered the body of Christ and legend describes them seeking revenge on those who display any disrespect.

This is illustrated wonderfully in a story called 'The Priest and the B-Men', which was recorded in Enniskillen, County Fermanagh in 1960. It describes a time when one of the main security forces, the Ulster Special Constabulary (USC), had checkpoints along the border in Northern Ireland. The USC were also known as the B-Specials and sometimes referred to as B-Men.

The story goes that a priest, who was a beekeeper, was travelling by car to visit a sick parishioner. Five miles out, he came to the customary checkpoint at the border and was ordered to stop and disembark from his vehicle. An officer, or B-Special, searched his car and then searched the priest's person. At this point, the priest objected, informing the B-Special that he was carrying the blessed sacrament in his breast pocket and requested that he demonstrate respect and cease examining his person. The officer rejected the priest's plea, reminding him of his stature and influence as one of the B-Men. Calmly, the priest acknowledged the officer's status, but informed him that this would carry little weight with his perceptive bees. In fact, he warned him that his loyal bees would eventually be the death of the B-Special.

The next morning, the officer, who was the owner of a big farm in the locality, awoke to discover his home blanketed in bees. Bees filled every crevice and thrummed against the chimney walls. With this, smoke filled the officer's home, forcing him outside to remedy the bee invasion. He balanced a ladder at the gable end and attempted to dislodge the web of bees, but to no avail. The swarm prevailed and solidified as one unit in defiance. The officer's ladder shook beneath him from his efforts. It wobbled from side to side until eventually the officer could no longer hold fast. He let go and fell to his death, being killed instantly upon impact. It is said that once the man's body was removed for burial, the bees disbanded immediately. As predicted by the priest, the bees were the death of the B-Special. They dutifully defended their keeper's honour and punished the man who disrespected him and the Blessed Eucharist.

This affiliation between the bees and the blessed sacrament is a recurring motif in folklore and aptly depicts the divine association with bees. Folk memory fondly describes bees acquiring the eucharist and embedding it in the heart of the hive, around which they construct an intricately built altar of wax in reverence. On occasion, the bees are heard humming in unison, similar to a church choir.

A fifteenth-century Irish manuscript, a translation of a Latin text written centuries earlier, contains a folktale entitled 'The Priest and the Bees'. It describes a priest embarking on a house call to give a dying man his last blessing with the sacred host. On his journey, he happens upon a thriving swarm of bees. The priest places the eucharist on the ground and proceeds to collect the swarm. In his distraction, he forgets the original aim of his journey as he hastens home to rehouse the swarm. Unbeknownst to him, he has left the holy eucharist behind. When the bees sense the absence of the host, they rise and return to the side of the road. There, they erect a chapel of wax around the host to protect and honour it. They adorn the wax chapel with a chalice and a pair of priests sculpted in wax, one on either side.

In folktales such as these, the hive itself becomes a place of worship, where the bees become the devotees, directing their reverence to the altar of wax. Unsurprisingly, lore also draws a parallel between the queen bee and a bishop, both presiding over their communities from a respected position of authority. Thomas of Centimpré – a Flemish Catholic medieval writer, preacher and theologian – wrote that a bishop could learn much from a queen bee, in terms of best practice and leadership, noting that as the leader of the hive does not use her sting, so too must a bishop exercise gentle authority.

Today, this sacred association is often celebrated around harvest time, when the farming season is drawing to an end, and honey is being extracted and is in strong supply. In Stoneleigh in Britain, a beekeepers' harvest festival is held annually at the beginning of October. Originally a church service, it is now more a secular event. The festivities serve to honour food created and foraged from the land,

Today, this sacred association is often celebrated around harvest time, when the farming season is drawing to an end, and honey is being extracted and is in strong supply.

and to mark the end of the beekeeping season for another year. In fact, this celebration was known as the Beekeepers' Service, a vibrant feature of the beekeeping calendar since the twelfth century. The service welcomed a gathering of beekeepers from different parts of the country, who surrounded beehives while holding brass candlesticks. It is interesting that brass is the prescribed material, as it is also the metal of choice when effectively 'ringing the bees' or making a swarm settle (as will be explored in chapter 9). At the harvest festival, the hive – like an altar – is adorned with gifts of honey, which traditionally would be distributed by the vicar to local almshouses and care homes.

Wonderfully, even in our more secular society, the piousness of bees and their produce is celebrated to this day. We continue the tradition of according the honeybee a respect that is deserving of them. Such admiration seems logical when we consider all that they achieve day to day. They construct a perfectly formed hexagonal comb, create their own food store, communicate to one another via movement and operate a fully functioning society with an assigned leader and designated roles. Scientists have long considered tool use a mark of intelligence and have been able to train bees to pull a string to access a sugary reward. In Vietnam, bees have been witnessed using dung as a tool by smearing it across a hive's entrance to ward off attacks by giant hornets.

Unsurprisingly, lore depicts bees as the most intelligent of all the animal and insect kingdoms. Today, the honeybee is highly esteemed as the most precise and effective of all pollinators and we recognise that they are an essential component of the survival of the planet

Chapter Four

SAINT GOBNAIT

PATRONESS OF THE BEES

Saint Gobnait of Ballyvourney in west Cork is a fitting patroness of the celestial bee. Similar to a worker bee, Gobnait is a tenacious female, a fierce warrior, in fact. She is a protector of her people and a self-sacrificing provider to her flock. It could be said that Gobnait is the personification of the honeybee itself.

In folklore, Gobnait is presented as a multifaceted character, being both soldier and saint. Her motivation to become a reliable ruler, dedicated to safeguarding her community, begins with a visitation of angels who foretell her divine purpose in life. She becomes a discerning leader of the highest calibre, embodying the characteristics of a goddess who performs miracles and is worshipped by her loyal followers.

Before Christianity, it is possible that Gobnait was a female version or consort of the Celtic smith god, who is known in the Irish language as Goibhniu or Gobán. Goibhniu was the name of the ironworker, or smith, of the Tuatha Dé Danann and these connections have led to Saint Gobnait being claimed by ironworkers as their patroness also. Interestingly, the name Gobán also occurs as a saint's name in early Christian Ireland. She is believed to be a descendant of Conaire the Great, a high king of

Ireland. Her name takes a few variations, from Gobnaith and Gobonett to Gubenta and everything in between; but it is Gobnait that is most prevalent. The meaning of the name is 'bringer of joy', which was also the meaning given to the biblical name Abigail. Therefore, Abbey, Abina and Abigail are all considered to be English translations of the Irish name Gobnait.

Much of what is known about Gobnait comes from the oral tradition and so her exact date of birth is something of a mystery. Folk tradition, however, holds that she was born during the sixth century. Many counties in Ireland lay claim to her, including Cork, Kerry, Galway (Inis Oírr), Tipperary, Waterford and Clare, the latter being the county widely considered to be her birthplace. She is said to have travelled with her father from the Cliffs of Moher to the island of Inis Oírr. Kerry tradition describes her landing into Dún Chaoin (or Dunquin) from the Aran Islands and continuing her travels alone across Kerry and Cork. Gobnait is remembered in countless legends emanating from all these areas, and is still revered specifically in Cork and Kerry, where churches, statues and holy wells have been created in her honour and carry her name. Her feast day, 11 February, is celebrated annually in Cork and Kerry, and continues to grow in popularity. In 2024, Ballyvourney locals programmed a festival to celebrate Gobnait's feast day, and invited women named Gobnait, Abby or Abigail to come together and celebrate their namesake.

Legend has it that Gobnait was the daughter of a pirate, smuggler and thief, who lived his life on the sea. She was an only child, with no maternal influence, and was forced to join her father and his plundering seafaring crew. Lore describes Gobnait's shame and abhorrence of her father's dishonest way of life. She pleaded with him to change his ways, but he gave her no heed. Alone one day, Gobnait was divinely admonished to flee the company of her wicked father and prepare herself for a nobler life. In this apparition, she was told to travel over the hills of Muskerry until she reached her place of 'resurrection' or '*port a h-eiséirí*' where nine white deer would be sleeping in a field. Here,

As an abbess, Gobnait soon became known as a strong, righteous and worthy protector of her convent and her people.

she was to erect her first church, or cell, and devote herself to a more pious way of life. White deer are inextricably connected with Gobnait during her younger years. The deer represent a place of refuge and solace. Like Saint Patrick, who transformed himself and his followers into a herd of deer to escape an ambush, so too does Gobnait appear in the guise of a white deer. Legend describes Gobnait metamorphosing into a deer for her protection, and being seen to graze amongst her sisters, also in the guise of white deer. To this day, symbols of white deer appear throughout Saint Gobnait's cemetery and shrine in Ballyvourney, adorning the railings and iron gates.

It is at Ballyvourney that Gobnait is first appointed abbess of a convent founded by Saint Abban. Son of the King of Leinster, Abban is said to have met Gobnait during his travels and been instantly drawn to her virtuous nature. As an abbess, Gobnait soon became known as a strong, righteous and worthy protector of her convent and her people. Similar to Saint Modomnoc, who reared his bees within the confines of his monastery, Gobnait also creates space for an apiary at her convent. She nurtures them daily, and an unyielding bond develops between the keeper and her bees. It is a symbiotic relationship where the bees also tend to Gobnait, becoming her defender and protector.

Warfare is a common theme in the legends associated with the saint. A favourite of mine is the story that describes Gobnait transforming her bees into human form and creating a band of soldiers to combat her enemy. She takes on the role of the queen bee, the matriarch of the hive and a fierce leader in battle. Gobnait possesses the special gift of communicating directly with her bees and ordering them to sting and attack the enemy, who instantly flee in the face of the bees' wrath. In other legends, Gobnait uses bees as her weaponry, and hurls skeps of bees directly at the enemy.

Tales relating to these battles are often found intertwined with narratives of Irish people being driven out of their homes by landlords, such as the Bodyke Evictions of the 1880s in County Clare. Gobnait comes to the rescue of her people in response to their prayers for help. In an instant, a swarm of bees appears and descends, fighting off the landlords. When Gobnait herself appears, she is described as a tall woman dressed in a long brown cloak with a skep, or straw hive, in her hand, poised for battle. Once there is victory, the vision of the saint quickly disappears.

The motif of bees manifesting as artillery is not unique to the story of Gobnait. There are several stories that describe bees being used in battle, some of which are of classical origin. German troops used bees to attack the British during the First World War (1914–1918). Soldiers are said to have concealed hives in dense, bushy areas and attached them skilfully to tripwires, serving as booby traps. The British army were exposed when they triggered the tripwires, provoking the bees and being stung. The sixteenth-century English poet and dramatist John Lyly was not wrong when he cautioned: 'The Bee that hath hunny in hir mouth, hath a sting in hir tayle' ('The bee that hath honey in her mouth, hath a sting in her tail').

Virgil also depended on his bees as a means of protection. It is said that when thieves attempted to steal from his property, he collected all his worldly possessions together and concealed them in the underbelly of his apiary. When the intruders approached, the bees were stirred into an angry swarm and attacked the thieves, who never again returned.

Another story of classical origin describes the fate of Zeus, whose life was under threat by his father, the Titan Kronos, king of the cosmos in Greek's so-called Golden Age. It was prophesied to Kronos that one of his children would eventually be responsible for his dethroning. Ruthless in character, Kronos worked towards circumventing this fate. He proceeded to devour five of his sons and daughters whole. His distraught wife, Rhea, was determined to save the life of one child. To this end, she substituted a stone wrapped in swaddling clothes in place of baby Zeus and moved him to the safety of a nearby cave where he was guarded by warriors. During this time, Zeus was tenderly nurtured by the sweetest of honey cultivated by the most sacred of bees. Hearing rumours of Zeus' hiding, enterprising locals began searching for Kronos' son, in the hope of receiving a reward. They approached the mouth of the cave ready to kidnap Zeus, but their efforts were quickly thwarted. The protective bees arose and attacked the intruders, stinging their eyes, entering their mouths and causing them to flee. When Zeus grew to manhood, he revolted and fulfilled the prophesy by dethroning his father, becoming king of the Greek gods.

We do not need to go as far back as the Golden Age to find evidence of the phenomenon of beekeepers summoning their bees to their defence. In January 2022, bees were used by Chilean protestors demonstrating against their government's management of the honey industry. Beekeepers brought around sixty hives to the demonstration and placed them in front of Chile's presidential palace. Many police officers were reportedly stung by the bees, and four beekeepers were detained. It is easy to imagine Saint Gobnait's satisfaction in beholding such a scene.

While Saint Patrick is known to have had a powerful crozier and Saint Brigid a miraculous cloak, Gobnait is often described as having her own unique instrument

While Saint Patrick is known to have had a powerful crozier and Saint Brigid a miraculous cloak, Gobnait is often described as having her own unique instrument on her person: a brass helmet, or a brass bell, from within which she conjures her bees.

on her person: a brass helmet, or a brass bell, from within which she conjures her bees. Legend describes a western chieftain of the O'Herlihy family beseeching Gobnait to assist them in recovering cattle stolen by O'Donoghue of the Glens in County Kerry. She listened with sympathy and considered his request. She told the chieftain that she would help him on the condition that he promised to become a Christian. As soon as he accepted the request, to his astonishment, he saw a goodly band of soldiers emerge, fit to win any battle. Saint Gobnait presented O'Herlihy with the brass helmet, which would be the instrument that provided him with protection in any future battle, as well as being a cure for fevers and epidemics.

Gobnait, like many Irish saints, is known for her healing powers. Since the eighteenth century, countless prayers have been dedicated to her with a direct request for a cure. The most common of these can be found at the base of Gobnait's statue, beside her shrine in Ballyvourney. The statue presents the saint stoically standing on a skep of bees, rosary beads draped across her praying hands, with the following prayer carved in stone beneath her:

Go mbeannaí Dia dhuit, a Ghobnait Naofa.
Go mbeannaí Muire dhuit agus beannaím féin duit;
Is chughat a thánag ag gearán mo scéil leat,
Is a d'iarraidh mo leigheas or son Dé ort!

May God and Mary bless you,
O Holy Gobnait and I bless you too;
And I come to you with my complaint,
and ask you for a cure in the name of God.

Variations of this prayer abound, where individuals have tailored their request to a specific ailment in need of a cure. In the early eighteenth century, for example, this was often an appeal for a cure for smallpox. It was well known that the efficacy of the cure would be greatly heightened if one opted to do the five stations as part of a 'round' at Gobnait's shrine in Ballyvourney. The tradition of this 'round' is still observed on Gobnait's feast day, 11 February. Station one begins at Gobnait's house, with two 'rounds' or clockwise circuits of the house being made by pilgrims, with intervals for prayers. The second station has two further stops for prayer, with rotations around Gobnait's grave. Stations three and four take place around Gobnait's church. Another custom at the church involves touching a stone ball – a bulla – lodged in an alcove of the church's external wall and making a wish or saying a prayer. Many use a handkerchief and retain the cloth for its healing qualities. The final station is known as the priest's grave, marking the burial place of Father Daniel O'Herlihy, with three stops alongside rounds of prayers. Following all eleven passages, people are encouraged to visit Gobnait's well, positioned a stone's throw away, outside the church grounds.

Holy wells in Ireland are famously revered for their curing potential, and this holds true for wells in Gobnait's name located in Cork and Kerry. Drinking water from the well is believed to grant good health. It was said that the water offers an ablution, a spiritual cleanse, as well as a cure for deep-seated disease. Offerings, such as coins or holy medals, are left as tokens of gratitude.

My first visit to Gobnait's Well in Ballyvourney was in 1999, with a fellow-folklorist, Christina Brophy. At this time, the entire holy well was brimming with devotions. Coins carpeted the well's base and countless rosary beads adorned an overhead tree branch, with holy medals, religious statues and prayer cards carefully positioned around the well's edge. What I was not expecting was to find medicinal items left beside the well, including an asthma inhaler, a pair of glasses and a single crutch. I wondered if the placement of these items signified that Gobnait was being called upon for assistance or whether she was deemed to have answered specific prayers. For heightened spiritual benefit, Ballyvourney locals used to recommend doing twenty-one rounds over twenty-one consecutive days. If you were fortunate enough to see a trout in the well at the end of the stations, this guaranteed that all your ailments and disease would be cured for the year ahead.

Devotees continue to congregate and pray for the souls of the dead, asking the saint to look over and protect them.

Twenty years after my first visit to Saint Gobnait's Church in west Cork, Dad and I revisited her reputed resting place in Ballyvourney in 2020. It was heartwarming to witness the reverence offered to Gobnait to this day. Devotees continue to congregate and pray for the souls of the dead, asking the saint to look over and protect them. All the offerings, including rosary beads and holy medals, had been removed. The iron gates, however, were beautifully decorated with figures of cast-iron deer. In 2024, I celebrated Gobnait's feast day in Ballyvourney and joined over a hundred visitors and locals to drink water from her well. The tree and holy well were once again decorated with ribbons, rosary beads and personalised offerings.

In Dún Chaoin, County Kerry, the remains of Saint Gobnait's Church, *Cill Ghobnait*, and a very special holy well, *Tobar Ghobnatan*, are positioned in the most majestic of settings at the cliff's edge, nestled into the landscape at the most westerly tip of the Dingle Peninsula, overlooking the Blasket Islands. As my sister Sinéad lives in the area, this is a pilgrimage that my dad, sister and I regularly take together.

Locals of Dún Chaoin cite Saint Gobnait as the patron saint of this Gaeltacht village and they also celebrate her feast day. Traditionally, Blasket Islanders came back to the mainland to offer their respects to the saint on her feast day, completing rounds and pilgrim prayers between the church and well. When Dad, Sinéad and I visited recently, we had the ethereal cliff walk to ourselves. The horseshoe-shaped well could be easily overlooked. In its recess are coins and holy medals offered in gratitude for the holy water's healing power, which is reputedly particularly effective for curing toothache and sore bones. The well is adorned by a stone carving in a likeness of Gobnait, which serenely gazes into the sacred spring. As Dad flipped a coin into the well's basin, I asked him what it was he wished for. He said he prayed for the safety of his four daughters and for the well-being of all his little bees.

Although the exact year of Gobnait's death is unknown, it is presumed to be during the sixth century. In Kerry and Cork, she is honoured on her feast day specifically, but other counties, including Galway, Waterford and Limerick, celebrate their proud association with the patroness of bees all year round. In Ballyvourney, a thirteenth-century wooden icon of the saint resides in Gobnait's Church. It is customary to kiss the wooden icon on 11 February and attach 'measures' or ribbons around it. The ribbons, known as '*tomhas Ghobnatan*' or Gobnait's measure, could be stowed away and used to safeguard against disease for the year ahead.

The following verse encapsulates much of what Saint Gobnait is remembered and respected for:

Saint Gobnait, Patroness of the Bees

Ag Baile Mhuirne tá buadh ar gach baile
Beatha Gobnait Naofa
Go mbíonn na sluaite daoine ann ag cantaireacht
Ag tabhairt a dturas in aghaidh an lae ann –
Do dhéin saighdiúirí as na beacaibh,
Is do thug dóibh airm ghléasta
Is do scaip an phláigh le naofacht.

At Ballyvourney which is better than all other towns
The life of holy Gobnait
Crowds of people chanting are there,
Offering pilgrimages day after day –
Making soldiers out of bees
Giving them armoury
Destroying plagues with her holiness.

(National Folklore Collection)

Chapter Five

A HOMAGE TO HONEY

Honeybees and their honey are symbolically imprinted in our imagination. They hold a position of value not only in scriptures, but also in ritual, folkloric customs and religious ceremonies. Outside the divine domain, the work of the bee has fascinated the greatest minds since the earliest civilisations. 'Whether it is that this liquid is the sweat of the heavens, or whether a saliva emanating from the stars, or a juice exuding from the air while purifying itself, would that it had been, when it comes to us, pure, limpid, and genuine, as it was, when first it took its downward descent.' So wrote Pliny the Elder in his *Natural History* around AD 77. He, along with many other philosophers, naturalists and scientists, including Virgil (70–19 BC) and Aristotle (384–322 BC), was intrigued by the matriarchy of the beehive, which has inspired innumerable studies. While some research contributed to improved beekeeping practices, other studies generated further confusion. This bewilderment gave rise to folklore that both emphasised and marvelled at how the bee's intelligence could outsmart even the most learned among us.

The bee and its produce have also inspired great artists, poets, writers and playwrights. In verse and song, bees and honey are both metaphor and muse. The hive is suggestive of the most harmonious and accomplished of societies, and honey is used as a symbol of life and a metaphor for love. The word honey in itself has become a synonym for a sweetheart or beloved. All that is sweet, wholesome and pure is encapsulated in this one rare gift created by bees in nature, resulting in a universal homage to honey.

Honey has long been described as the food of the gods. In early Irish literature, Manannán – the mythical Son of Lir – describes the land of promise as flowing with streams of honey. Tír na nÓg was described by Niamh to Oisín as a place abundant in honey and wine and without any trace of death or decay. One of Ireland's most celebrated high kings, Cormac mac Airt, was renowned for hosting tremendous feasts in the banqueting hall at Tara, named *Teach Míodhchuarta*, or the Mead Circling House, a hall for feasting and celebration. His name is associated in Irish folklore with a golden era in Ireland, one of splendour and prosperity, a land bountiful with honey.

Before we learned how to extract sugar from sugar cane, around AD 600, honey held pride of place as the original sweetener. In addition to being a primary food ingredient, honey was discovered to be an invaluable medicinal aid, being a natural antiseptic. In history and folklore, honey is used as a curing agent. For all these reasons, honey has been revered and it was integrated into ceremonial rituals and blessings and is ubiquitously esteemed in history, philosophy, science, literature and folklore.

In our household, honey was always referred to as 'the liquid gold', as every drop has its value. Dad is a master at extracting every last morsel of sweet goodness from each honeycomb, which instilled in us a respect for the bee's labour. It is said that the lifetime work of a single bee amounts to one teaspoonful of honey. It was the anticipation of collecting his own honey that enticed Dad to start keeping bees. His neighbour Joe Doyle gave him and his older brother, Jim, their first 'nuc' (pronounced 'nuck') or nucleus colony of bees. Folklore suggests this to be the most appropriate way of transferring ownership of bees from one person to another, considering it somewhat crass to have money pass hands when dealing with the noble bee. To this end, Dad is quite proud of never having paid base money for bees in his lifetime.

Dad remembers the same neighbour from his childhood, Joe Doyle, generously gifting the household a biscuit tin full of honey at the end of each beekeeping season. In a family of eight, the liquid gold did not last long and so my father and his brother set their sights on creating their own honey supply, which came to fruition one year later. At the age of fourteen, Dad sold honey for the first time, to Rowans, a Dublin grocer who came to Wexford to hold a honey market annually. He sold 1 lb of honey for one shilling and sixpence, and made £7 that day. Dad was reared hearing 'If you can't make it, you can't have it'; his response was to become a beekeeper and ensure that sweetness would be in full supply from that year onwards.

While bees do not need a keeper or require the intervention of the human hand at any stage of honey production, a proficient beekeeper can positively influence the temperament and productivity of a hive. With year-round feeding and monitoring, a keeper can contribute towards building stronger hives, resulting in higher honey yields. The location of an apiary, as chosen by the keeper, will influence the flavour of honey produced. Box hives, with moveable frames, provide consistent shelter for the bees throughout the year. However, none of these factors will prevent or deter the work of the bees. Ultimately, bees do not need us. Seasonal change and access to flowers and plants are the main factors that determine the beginning, end and outcome of a beekeeping season.

The creation of honey is a testament to the high functionality of the bee workforce, each bee having its own individual role and responsibility in the hive. It is the forager bee that leaves the hive and collects nectar from flowers, trees and bushes. She returns to the hive and passes the nectar onto the house bees. Even on her return flight, she begins to dilute the nectar with her saliva, which contains enzymes that assist in the transformation of nectar into honey. When the forager returns to the hive, there is further movement, which is fondly described as the bees' waggle or wagtail dance. It brings me pure joy knowing that bees communicate through the medium of dance! They transfer information, such as where nectar is located and its distance from the hive, and communicate this using their own bespoke, embodied and visual language.

After the dance, the forager bee passes little pockets of nectar to the house bee. This is the last step of the process and is a sight to behold. They appear head to head, as if in fierce debate, and using their probosces, or tongues, pass nectar from one bee to the other. During this transfer, the antennae of both bees, like rigorous hand gestures, are in a flurry of continuous motion. The nectar is manipulated into sucrose as it is incubated in the house bee's mouth. The bee ingests and regurgitates the nectar, mixing it with an enzyme called invertase. This enzyme converts the sucrose into the two main sugar constituents of honey – fructose and glucose – until finally, the mixture is lodged into the honeycomb. The cells are then capped with a thin flake of wax which the bee excretes from glands on her underbelly. With the correct incubation time of about three to four days, and at the optimum temperature of between 30 and 35 degrees centigrade, the nectar becomes honey.

The forager bee performs one of two accomplished movements that communicates to other foragers where food is located and where the most plentiful bounty can be found. The choreography of the dance has two distinct formations. The round dance indicates that food is within approximately ninety metres of the hive. This is expressed by the worker bee dancing to the left and then pivoting to the right. Some of her audience make contact with her as she moves. As the dancer is cloaked in the scent of the flower, which has lingered on her furry body, the surrounding bees absorb the smell which will orientate their foraging once they leave the hive. The abundance of food is expressed by the tempo of the dance. The more rapid the movement, the more plentiful the hoard.

The wagtail or waggle dance is more intricate and communicates technical information with ease. The dancer moves in a straight line up the honeycomb, wagging the tail end of her rump back and forth. She then circles back, without moving her tail, until she returns to her starting position. The dance commences again, with movement in a straight line, until she tapers off, this time to the left, looping back to her starting point. The number of times she wags her rump along the straight line indicates the distance between the hive and the food source. The more sluggish the waggle, the farther away the nectar is located.

The sun is their spotlight, and they use its location to indicate the direction they must orientate their flight. If the dancer moves directly towards the sun, this means the food is straight ahead. If movement diverges at an angle, this illustrates the distance from the sun the bee must fly. As the position of the sun shifts, so too do the angle and orientation of the dance. Information is creatively generated and shared between them, movement by movement and moment to moment.

> … Even the pollen-drunk dance of the messenger
> returned from gardens heavy with blossoms
> is a kind of mathematical waltz, calculating
> in each step the sun's slow orbit through
> the heavens …
>
> ('The Beekeeper to His Assistant', Noel Duffy)

The duration of time that the nectar remains in the comb, combined with the correct temperature of the hive, as regulated by the fanning of the bees' wings, is essential for the transformation of nectar into honey. In addition, the moisture content of the hive needs to be low to ensure the nectar remains fresh. Nectar will go bad unless most of the water has evaporated, which makes the sugar content of honey extremely high. This high sugar content creates an intolerable environment for yeasts and bacteria to multiply, making honey a natural antiseptic – yet another prized attribute of the honeybees' produce. In fact, archaeologists have found pots of honey buried in Ancient Egyptian tombs that are over 3,000 years old and the honey is deemed to be perfectly edible still.

As well as being sterile, honey is also highly nutritious, containing organic acids, protein and amino acids, as well as the minerals phosphorus, calcium, iron and vitamins A, B (B1, B2 and B6) and C. This nutritional goodness is mostly the result of the bees' enzymes being added to the nectar at the early stages of honey production. Honey has rightfully been documented as having the ability to protect people from infection and disease.

During the First World War, honey was reportedly used by soldiers in the trenches to prevent infections, reduce inflammation and accelerate the healing process. In the

1970s, doctors in Britain were said to have 'rediscovered' the germ-fighting properties of honey, using it as a dressing for infected operation wounds. Enzyme activity, combined with honey's acidity, aids the formation of its antibacterial properties.

As is often the case with folklore, stories describing the healing attributes of honey are rooted in factual knowledge. Honey emerges as a popular folk cure for a myriad of illnesses and ailments. The most familiar use, to this day, is in fighting the common cold, flu and sore throats. Irish folk cures prescribe the addition of various, more unpredictable ingredients that will enhance honey's efficacy in this regard. In County Laois, it was recommended that the juice of a turnip be added to honey to ease a hoarse throat. For optimal results, a layer of honey should be placed between slices of turnip, leaving it to soak for an hour or two. The juice of the turnip combined with the honey created a thick syrup, and this was considered the perfect application for a scratchy throat.

Other folk recipes suggest blending honey with a variety of ingredients to combat cold or flu, such as one of the following: garlic, flaxseed, lemon juice, the white of an egg, mustard or boiled milk. A little more unorthodox, perhaps, is the notion that honey can remedy baldness. Massaged thoroughly onto the scalp both night and day,

As is often the case with folklore, stories describing the healing attributes of honey are rooted in factual knowledge. Honey emerges as a popular folk cure for a myriad of illnesses and ailments.

it was considered a treatment for those who are follicly challenged! For heightened effect, it was suggested to combine the honey with dead bees and honeycomb to thicken the paste. Administering this in generous layers proved more efficacious still.

In a section dedicated to folk cures in the National Folklore Collection, UCD, honey emerges as a cure for all manner of illnesses. It is deemed effective for arthritis, psoriasis, chickenpox, gangrenous feet, thrush, boils, hay fever, whooping cough, thrush, rheumatism, cold sores, burns and bedsores. Rheumatism is also said to be alleviated and even cured from repeated bee stings. Accounts from Kildare and Limerick recommend intentionally interfering with beehives in order to get a 'good stinging' to relieve arthritic pain.

In Britain, a spoonful of honey at bedtime could safeguard against bed-wetting; but the honey used should be freshly scraped directly from the extractor, and were the honey to be heated, its curing properties would be lessened.

Honey, administered to animals, also cured and eased a range of ailments. In Wexford, it was deemed the ultimate cure and was effective at easing murrain (a fever) in cattle, old cuts and wounds. Its strength is in its ability to absorb the poisonous pus whilst simultaneously offering comfort to the infected area. In Cavan, honey was traditionally used on animals experiencing sore or scratchy eyes. It was a soothing remedy for head injuries and sinus complaints in horses, when mixed with oil, vinegar and mustard and administered to both nostrils. Domestic animals have also been reported to benefit from the healing qualities of honey. A man I had the pleasure of interviewing in 1999 shared that he used honey for treating his cats' illnesses, specifically as they were prone to abscesses. He rated honey's healing power highly and favoured the potential ingestion of honey to any synthetic ointment, as cats were sure to lick their wounds.

As we lived in a beekeeping household, honey was naturally the first antidote suggested, regardless of the complaint. It dressed grazed knees, eased burns and cuts and was smeared on gauze cloth and administered for eczema and psoriasis. Naturally, a large spoonful was administered with the first sniff of a cold: my aunt Marcella, Dad's sister, combined a drop of whiskey with honey, lemon and hot water, mixed into a syrup that was boiled on the hob. It always hit the spot. A significant disadvantage of growing up in a beekeeping household is that honey invariably turns up everywhere: on light switches, on door handles and other random objects. It was a given that accepting a lift in the car from Dad, specifically after a beekeeping trip to Wexford, meant bringing something to sit on or accepting that blobs of honey and wax would find their way onto your clothes.

The merits of honey have contributed to its heavenly, otherworldly status in lore and legend. There is a harmony between the celebration of the virtues of honey in Irish folklore and the reverence bestowed upon it in Greek and Roman times.

Historically, honey was integrated into a variety of rituals and celebrations, being the food of the gods. Today, the honeymoon is the most common celebration associated with honey. The term was coined due to the ancient custom of drinking mead after the wedding ceremony: honey wine was drunk by the married couple for an entire month, or moon cycle, immediately after the matrimonial rite, hence 'honeymoon'.

In ancient times, honey was incorporated into the matrimonial ceremony itself, being daubed on the bride's lips and placed on the doorway of the newly-weds' home. This assured prosperity and good fortune to the household and to the happy couple. If the sign of the cross was traced with honey on the threshold of a new home, this also ensured good luck and banished demons.

A Germanic tradition describes honey, akin to holy water, being used during baptismal ceremonies. It was smeared on the baby's lips and traced on the baby's forehead as a blessing ritual.

In Africa, the Maasai tribe are documented to have incorporated the brewing of honey wine as a ritual during the honeymoon itself. The custom involved the husband and wife brewing the liquid together in an isolated hut. It was strictly forbidden to have sexual intercourse during this time. In fact, it was essential that they remained chaste for two days before the brewing began, and for six full days while the process lasted. It was believed that if the couple breached the rule of chastity, the honey wine would be toxic and undrinkable, and the bees would abandon the household in revolt.

A Germanic tradition describes honey, akin to holy water, being used during baptismal ceremonies. It was smeared on the baby's lips and traced on the baby's forehead as a blessing ritual. This was also a source of protection for the baby, as newborns were regarded as a soul or spirit until they ingested food.

In Christianity, honey was deemed a symbolic agent of purification. Anointing the baby's lips with honey served as a precaution against a death occurring in the family. This tallies with Irish folk tradition, where honey was used as a defence against evil spirits.

In early Christian times, newborn babies were fed with honey immediately after birth, in the hope of enhancing their potential. Similar to the benefits imparted by bees congregating around a newborn in their cradle, such as that experienced by Saint Ambrose, patron saint of beekeepers, honey ingested by a baby was said to bestow gifts of eloquence, song and poetry.

In Irish lore, honey is the foodstuff of the fairies. In Fermanagh, the sap produced by plants found flourishing along the edges of streams and rivers is a sweet, honeylike substance called '*manna*', which has been integrated into folklore as a honey of sorts. It was considered to be an enriching food befitting the denizens of the otherworld. '*Manna*', deriving from the Irish word '*mana*', means a portent or a sign. In areas where '*manna*' is seen dripping from the underside of leaves, it is an indication that fairies were feasting on honey there the night before.

Poets, dramatists and novelists have been inspired by the humble bee for centuries. From Shakespeare to Sylvia Plath – whose death occurred coincidentally on Saint Gobnait's feast day – to singer-songwriter Richard Thompson, bees have inspired verse, song, literature and art. Even the boxer Muhammad Ali invoked bees when he claimed to 'float like a butterfly, sting like a bee'. Bees are symbolic of order and used as a metaphor for the best in human behaviour, representing industriousness and harmony. Seamus Heaney phrased it perfectly in his Nobel lecture in 1995, when he described the image of the honeybee as being 'deeply lodged in poetic tradition and always suggestive of the ideal of an industrious, harmonious, nurturing commonwealth'. And from this utopian environment, honey is created: fragrant, wholesome and pure.

I believe honey is deserving of the homage it has evoked. It has been deemed the food of the gods, a sacred secretion from heaven. Liquid gold has the capacity to heal and cure, to bless and protect. And today, its merits continue to be lauded. It is an acknowledgment of, and a tribute to, the universal love for the honeybee.

Chapter Six

BEESWAX AND HONEYCOMB

The revolutionary socialist Karl Marx, political theorist, philosopher and economist, described the phenomenon that is the bees' ability to create a perfectly formed hexagonal-shaped honeycomb, writing that 'a bee puts to shame many an architect in the construction of her cells.' Whilst architects have the advantage of being able to source readily available materials, bees generate their own raw material, producing the honeycomb wherein they live, work, reproduce and thrive.

The uniform hexagons that create the honeycomb lattice are nothing short of awe inspiring. If the cells were circular, gaps would form between each one, and although squares and triangles would be airtight, it is the hexagon that is the most space efficient and advantageous structure. The six-sided cells use the least material and support the greatest weight, making it the most effective, and arguably, the most appealing shape visually.

Honeycomb is made from wax produced by worker bees, for the most part. It is created by the ingestion of honey combined with chemicals secreted from the bees' abdomens. Scales of wax are transferred from their bellies up to their mouths for preparation, and it is estimated that it takes two tablespoonfuls of honey to make one ounce (28 grams) of wax. The queen uses wax for nesting purposes. She issues thin sheets of wax after egg laying is complete and creates a canopy where the larvae can be nursed. The worker bees place a lid of wax across each cell, keeping the larvae, pollen, nectar and honey protected and perfectly enclosed.

Towards the end of the beekeeping season, the hope is that combs will appear swollen with honey when taken from the hive. Beekeepers remove the wax caps from each comb using a scraper, an uncapping fork or a long-edged knife: Dad's preferred implement. There are few sounds more satisfying to me than hearing the cells being decapitated, and seeing the honey ooze from the comb.

Wax cappings are an invaluable by-product of the hive. Collecting it can be a messy process of squeezing, melting and straining with gauze cloths and strainers, but the end result – wax cakes – has been a versatile commodity used for centuries.

Frequently, beekeepers will recycle wax by repurposing it within the hive itself and adding it to the honeycomb foundations. Dad ensures that nothing is wasted from the work of the bee, using every by-product of the hive in some shape or form. To this end, he places all the removed cappings into a large homemade metal box with a glass covering. This moveable container is a permanent feature in our back garden, perched on the shed's roof, to make the most of the melting potential of the Irish sun. The principle of the apparatus rests on the double-glazed lid conserving heat. The metal enclosure is propped at an oblique angle so that the melting wax will slide to the bottom and collect at the box's base. This approach, using what is often called a solar wax melter, is adopted by most beekeepers.

Over the last ten years or so, Dad has frequently been approached by people asking for wax cakes, owing to the upsurge in organic and natural ingredients, such as beeswax, being incorporated into beauty products, skincare and cosmetics. Recently, he was approached by an asthma patient, who maintained that ingesting beeswax with a little honey, and spitting it out after a good chew, greatly improved his respiratory issues.

As wax is made from honey, it is imbued with all the natural goodness an antiseptic substance provides. Traditionally, beeswax was commonly used for a variety of cures for burns, ear pain, warts, blisters, splinters and even ringworm. It was also effective for a toothache or for filling a cavity, and wax wrapped in a cloth and tied around one's head would cure any level of headache.

The following recipe, written in 1959 and sourced from a Galwegian beekeeper, gives precise directions for creating the perfect treatment for burns, using beeswax and herbs from the garden, including the *nóinín* or daisy, dock leaves, described as 'docket' below, and bark from an elder tree:

> When the honey was taken from the combs, her mother used the wax that remained as a basis for burn ointment. She boiled the combs, from which she first soaked out the honey. She then left the water grow cold in which she boiled the empty combs. When the water got cold, a lair [layer] of wax was left on top of the water. Then she got the roots of the *nóinín* [daisy], the roots of the weed known as docket, and the bark of the elder tree ... These then were all pounded up and mixed with unsalted butter. The bees-wax from the boiled combs was mixed through. Mrs. McDonnell said it made a very good skin ointment for burns.
>
> (National Folklore Collection)

Apart from its impressive curative properties, beeswax being used for candles has been a primary repurposing of one of the hive's natural resources. Beeswax has the highest melting point of any wax, and so it will burn for longer. Social commentary on life and practices in ancient Ireland often describes poorer folk relying on rush candles and paraffin oil, whilst beeswax was a staple in houses of the rich or the well-to-do.

Wax candles have inspired a rich canon of traditions and beliefs in Irish folklore. Candles – as a cure, as signs of luck and misfortune and as portents of wisdom and truth – are at the core of some interesting folk rituals. Fundamentally, it was believed that candles transferred a message, or inherited a meaning, by the flicker of the flame or the way it burned and melted. The candle represents illumination in all its guises, revealing truths and imparting guidance.

The patterns or shapes formed by melted wax were seen to present the formation of a story, and the motions of a glimmering flame could foretell the future. It could predict a letter arriving in the post, as seen in this quote from the National Folklore Collection, which was recorded in Cavan in 1942: 'If there was a little spark at the butt of the wick of the lit candle, the people would say: "There is a letter on the candle. There is a letter coming to the house!" I saw it myself, a hundred times, and I found it to be true every time.'

If a flame ignited a spark, this was perceived as a token of good luck. On the contrary, misfortune – death, in fact – was destined if a candle burned unevenly. A similar fate was determined if wax melted in one continuous flow without breaking, or if a halo or shroud appeared to be glowing around the candle's flame.

Being able to decipher the message, or 'read the candle', was considered a special gift. A candle reader could extrapolate deeper insight and knowledge by interpreting the flame and the melting wax. People requested this service: that a candle be burned for them and their fortune, or misfortune, told.

A story recounted from County Antrim describes a woman gifted in the art of candle reading. Her approach involved identifying the silhouettes of saints that formed within the melted wax. Saints Patrick, Brigid and Colmcille all appeared to her. Once she had deciphered the shape of the specific saint, her client was told to devote their prayers accordingly and their sins would be forgiven. The same reader also assisted in the identification of one's future partner, offering guidance to a lovelorn woman who had not yet met her match. The reader dropped wax into a keyhole and waited for it to reveal its guidance, and in the shapes that formed, the initials of the young woman's future partner were identified.

Integrating candles into calendar customs is a beloved tradition in Irish and other folk traditions. Lighting a candle and leaving it on a windowsill on Christmas Eve was said to illuminate the path for the holy family of the infant, Mary and Joseph, should they be looking for a night's shelter. Ireland's first female president, Mary

Robinson, reignited this tradition in 1990 when she committed to placing a lit candle in the window of Áras an Uachtaráin, the president's official residence. The light was a symbolic beacon that welcomed home returning emigrants and diaspora.

The custom of placing a candle on the table on Christmas night to encourage great blessings for the family in the coming year was popular in Kerry. It was also recommended to eat breakfast on Christmas morning by candlelight to ensure good luck for the ensuing year. At Easter, it was customary for the father of a household to light a candle and bless the four corners of his house, hearth and threshold with Easter holy water. A tradition at Halloween involved lighting two candles and placing them on either side of the fireplace. If they burned clear, good luck would follow, but if they sparked, misfortune was destined.

The ceremonial candles that feature most often in folklore are blessed candles such as those used for wakes, which held heightened significance and were believed to provide spiritual guidance. Candles made from beeswax were afforded an additional benefit by the local priest who blessed the candles on Candlemas Sunday. Candlemas – a Christian celebration still observed annually on 2 February – refers to the ritual of blessing candles. It is a day symbolic of purification and light. The priest's blessing enhanced the ability of the beeswax candle to cure illness and safeguard the home against evil spirits and misfortune. For this reason, blessed candles were cherished, and never allowed to be burned to the end.

In addition to the supply of light and guidance offered by beeswax in its candle form, there are countless other practical and innovative uses for bees' produce. The people I interviewed tell of furniture polish being the most popular use of beeswax traditionally. Nothing needs to be added or adapted, just beeswax gently softened with heat, applied with a cotton cloth and administered to wooden furniture. Using a steady and even hand, apply a few layers for a depth of colour and a natural protective finish. A recipe for floor polish, from the 1970s, suggests a few added extras: 2 ounces (50 grams) of candle-ends, 4 ounces of beeswax and 2 ounces of soap dissolved in a teaspoonful of water, with a pint of turpentine.

Folk memory recalls an assortment of other traditional household uses, such as adding beeswax to feather pillows to prevent the quills from scratching and using it as a seal for letters, or as a cap for sealing bottles of beer. In more affluent households, beeswax was sprinkled amongst luxurious fabrics, such as lace and silk, to maintain and protect it from acquiring a yellow hue.

Overarchingly, the ancillary uses of beeswax are a triumph, but arguably, there is another jewel in the crown.

As Karl Marx noted, bees can be regarded as outsmarting architects by virtue of their ability to produce the comb, in a specific shape, without forward planning or use of a drawing. In fact, the creation of hexagonal prisms demonstrates bees devising a design solution. This adaptation was analysed by Charles Darwin during his research into evolutionary theory in the 1850s.

Darwin recognised the importance of bees evolving comb-building abilities, which in short pointed to their governing intelligence. To investigate further, Darwin carried out experiments to test, analyse and decipher the work of the bee. Like the thinkers and writers who preceded him, such as Aristotle – who is renowned in bee lore – Darwin concluded that bees are the most wonderful of all insects. For Darwin, this was demonstrated by their natural engineering skills and honeycomb production, which is created from their self-made wax. This feat of construction was achieved by bees using their instinct and intelligence. He realised that the evolution of the bees' comb-building abilities was essential if his theory on natural selection was to be taken seriously. These little insects evolved to solve a design issue by adopting the best shape in which to work, live and prosper.

In science and naturalism, the work of the bee has incited intrigue, triggered research and influenced society and theoretical thinking. In folklore, this awe and fascination has been embedded into legend. This is the fertile bedrock of lore where the bee consistently emerges as the most intelligent of all creatures, never failing to overcome obstacles and challenging even the most learned in society.

Chapter Seven

ARISTOTLE AND THE BEES

As well as leading the Irish Literary Revival and co-founding the Abbey Theatre, Lady Augusta Gregory was a keen collector of stories and lore in her local town of Coole, County Galway. During her fieldwork, she learned that the name Aristotle was synonymous with wisdom, being told by the wife of one of the estate's labourers, when a bee flew in through an open door, that 'Aristotle of the books was very wise, but the bees got the best of him in the end'. His name conjures a character that is most learned, intelligent and wise.

The folktale of Aristotle and the bees is one of my personal favourites. In it, the pioneering philosopher, scientist, inventor and naturalist is outsmarted by the bees. Commonly told in the form of a triad, the folktale describes three phenomena that Aristotle tried but failed to understand: the ebb and flow of the tide, a woman's mind and the work of the bee. It tells how Aristotle experimented relentlessly to learn how bees created honey. In all variations of the tale, the bees not only deny him access to the knowledge he so desperately craves but get the better of him at every turn.

The folktale aligns with the recurring motif in bee lore: that this insect is the most intelligent and superior of all creatures. Being the epitome of wisdom, bees continually outwit us mere mortals. The magical essence of this story, however, derives from the unique characteristics it has inherited, being shared orally and passed from one generation to the next, through storytelling. This is a popular folktale in Ireland, with lovely nuances emerging within versions collected in Kerry, Louth, Waterford, Cork and Galway. In an account from County Tipperary, we are told that the cleverest man in the land was named Harry Steaitle, whose name has been converted, through storytelling, from Aristotle, and so a new character named Harry has been generated through folklore.

The story has been embellished with colourful detailing over time. Another great example of this comes from County Cork, in an account recorded in 1936. Our protagonist is now Harry Stattle, a clever man who is shamed by the bees. In this account, Harry Stattle is described as smug in character, by considering himself the cleverest of all men. He was smart, with great wit, and was also the best huntsman of his time. He was said to own fourteen dogs, named Fifo, Fiddler, Juno, Jiggle, Fido, Fanny, Farmer, Spanker, Spoker, Tanner, Joker, Dido, Miller and Ranger. As smart as he was, the work of the bees remained an enigma to him. He was tormented by the mysterious workings of the hive.

To demystify the bees, Harry decided to build a glass box and observe them at work. A day later, he was shocked when he returned to his experiment to discover that the disgruntled bees had smeared the inside of the glass with wax to thwart his scrutiny. He was infuriated. In his anger, he kicked over the glass box, smashing it to pieces.

The bees escaped, arose and swarmed around Harry, stinging him to such an extent that he was left blind. In self-loathing and despair, Harry abandoned his home and went into exile. He could not rid himself of the shame of being outsmarted by mere insects and his reputation being destroyed. After much journeying, Harry reached a *botháinín* (a little hut) in which lived three *seandraoise* (old people), named Tadhg an Dá Mhaide, Tadhg an Dá Veast and Tadhg an Dá Dhroinn. Even here, in this desolated hut, Harry could not escape mockery and shame. The head of the house, Tadhg an Dá Mhaide, taunted him relentlessly until the end of his days about how the cleverest of all men was outwitted by the little bees.

Variations of this folktale, with bespoke characteristics, have been collected nationally. In another version from County Cork, we are introduced to Nanisteacil, rather than Harry Stattle. This version picks up on the language of the bees before they swarm, just before the glass hive is kicked over and demolished. The storyteller marvels that '*bhí a gcaint féin acu eatarthu féin*' (they had their own language between them).

An account from Kerry introduces Aristotle as the brother of a well-known local woman from Dún Chaoin. He is visiting his sister, having travelled over from London to see her. Whilst there, he pursues his quest of deciphering the work of the bees. As expected, his efforts are futile and he is described as being left as *dall*, or blind, as ever. In this account he is left blind to the truth, rather than literally blind, as was the case in the Cork version of the tale.

The practice of observing bees using a glass box is a common and well-documented approach that is adopted to this day. For open days at Airfield Estate in Dundrum, Dad has presented bees in a glass case, displaying a single

The practice of observing bees using a glass box is a common and well-documented approach that is adopted to this day.

comb with a queen, alongside a team of worker bees. The beauty is getting up close to the action without the fear of being stung. The bees can be observed intimately at length as they work and move from cell to cell.

As is often the case in folklore, there is a basis in fact as to why Aristotle is connected to bees. Like Virgil and Darwin, Aristotle was fascinated by how a hive operated and honey was created. To learn more, he carried out extensive research and documented his findings. Over his lifetime, Aristotle produced research papers across a range of subject areas – on justice, on the soul, on the sciences, on species and genus, on animals (in nine books), on plants and more – but it was his work on the natural sciences, *The History of Animals*, that captured his observations of a generation of bees.

Aristotle's research methodology involved erecting a glass hive, as is presented in the folktale. His tactics were incorporated into a book of bee lore by an Arabic writer, Ad-Amiri, in 1371, whose writing was largely inspired by Aristotle and Virgil's analysis of bees. In this, Ad-Amiri describes Aristotle implementing an observational glass structure to facilitate his analysis of bee life.

Although Aristotle engaged with beekeepers during his fieldwork, much of his study was theoretical rather than practical and so some unfounded hypotheses appear in his research. His theory pertaining to the origin of honey pre-empted Pliny the Elder's thinking. Aristotle claimed in *The History of Animals* (Book V) that 'Honey falls from the air, principally at the rising of the stars, and when the rainbow rests upon the earth.' He described bees being created by the male ruler of the hive, the king bee. Interestingly, this misconception was not rectified for a further two thousand years, when the queen bee was rightfully recognised as matriarch of the hive.

In Aristotle's observation and documentation of the bees' activities, his genius is witnessed in his stream of questioning, proposals and counterproposals. He was miffed that female worker bees had the ability to sting, claiming that 'Nature does not assign defensive weapons to any female creature'. The work and order of bees incited a deep curiosity in Aristotle and challenged his beliefs about the natural order of things, such as females having the capacity to fight.

From the primitive to the most sophisticated of minds, bees have been seen as a supreme example of the miraculous and creative power of nature, and for this reason, bees have become the inspiration and alchemy of fables and folklore.

Chapter Eight

TELLING THE BEES

The tradition of 'telling the bees' is one of the most familiar and beloved rituals associated with bees. It is a profound enactment of the belief that bees should be told when significant events occur in the family of the beekeeper. The custom draws together several characteristics attributed to these little creatures: their gentle disposition, their perception and wisdom, and the idea that they have a sacred soul. The act of telling the bees is one of deep respect, and signals how highly they are regarded as an integral and valued part of a household. This custom is an exquisite illustration of the affinity that can exist between bees and their keeper, a bespoke bond born out of loyalty and respect.

The implication of this tradition is that bees are treated like extended members of the family. Although the custom largely involves sharing news of a death, it includes other special moments in a household, such as a birth or a marriage. It is considered the polite and appropriate action to take, and if it is not fulfilled, the bees are likely to take offence and demonstrate their wrath by either abandoning the hive, ceasing to produce honey or succumbing to death themselves. Telling the bees becomes a safeguard against losing a hive and serves to integrate the bees into the household.

This custom is most poignant when there is a death in the family, especially when it is the death of a beekeeper. In accordance with Ireland's strong tradition of honouring its departed by funeral rites and wakes, sharing news of a death with the bees is a custom that has been handed down orally and, wonderfully, it has survived to the present day.

In folklore, there are innumerable Irish traditions and customs associated with death. In rural and urban homes across Ireland, it is customary to wake our loved ones. We leave an open coffin in the front room and welcome in neighbours, day and night, to pay their respects, share memories, eat, drink and perhaps play a few tunes. Specific rituals are customary at this time. A friend of mine from Listowel, County Kerry, was instructed by her mother to stop the clock and open the window when her time came. The open window releases the spirit from the home, and stopping the clock ensures that ample respect is given without the restriction of time, so as to properly mourn the loss. Traditionally, two persons from a household carried news of a death to neighbours, livestock and, very importantly, to the bees.

Telling the bees is a popular tradition across the four provinces of Ireland. An account recorded in Antrim in 1954, one of my personal favourites, describes a man by the name of Jimmy Bann, who was known for having a special connection with his bees. He tended to share all his news with them but when it came to telling them about the passing of his dear mother, he went to special efforts. He prepared himself by washing and shaving. He polished his Sunday boots and donned his best suit. Only then did he feel properly able to undertake the ceremony of telling the bees about his sad loss.

Although not a suit-wearing man, Dad makes it his business to wear his suit to funerals as a sign of respect for the deceased. When my mother passed away, he visited his beehives in Airfield Estate, Dundrum, to share the news of his broken heart. No paraphernalia was used in his delivery, just a few words spoken gently, with his large hands brushing the top of each wooden hive. At the time, I recall him saying that it was the right thing to do.

In folklore, failing to do the right thing can have its repercussions. In 1944, a Galwegian beekeeper lamented his failure to respect the custom and, in turn, how he paid the ultimate price: his bees withered away in their hives.

Bees can demonstrate their umbrage in other ways. In an account from 1959, another Galwegian, by the name of McCormack, had seventeen hives. He was known for his rapport with his bees, being able to hold them in the palm of his hand without ever being stung. When

McCormack died, however, no one informed his bees. The day his casket went up the hill, it is said that his bees dutifully followed the funeral procession en masse and never returned to their beehives.

I had the pleasure of interviewing a man who recounted a similar story. Donal McSweeney, from Macroom in County Cork, described how he witnessed bees following their keeper's funeral. While pointing to the roadway the funeral procession took, he explained that the man's bees followed him in a cloud overhead. Donal attempted to offer a reasonable explanation, admitting ''twas rather weird', but the reality remained: that the bees accompanied their keeper to his final resting place.

Two years later, I collected a similar story in County Cork. A woman from Ballydehob described how her

The day his casket went up the hill, it is said that his bees dutifully followed the funeral procession en masse and never returned to their beehives.

cousin's widow visited the grave of her deceased husband, a beekeeper, a few days after the burial. When she reached the grave, it was laden with bees and butterflies. My informant speculated that perhaps the funeral flowers had attracted the bees. However, she related that the beekeeper's wife believed that her husband's bees, which he had cared for so dearly, were paying their last respects and saying goodbye to their beloved keeper.

Telling the bees is a popular tradition that has been recorded in the US, UK and central Europe. In the US and the UK, the news is often delivered in the form of a rhyme, such as the following verse collected in Lincolnshire and quoted in the *British Bee Journal* in 1970:

Honey bees, honey bees, hear what I say!
Your master, J.A., has passed away.
But his wife now begs you will freely stay
And still gather honey for many a day
Bonny bees, bonny bees, hear what I say!

When recounting the news, people might also tap the tops of the beehives using a bunch of keys. English folk practice specifies that house keys should be used for this purpose. Another custom in England involved rotating the beehives when the corpse was being carried out of the house. It is as if the bees are being protected from the grievous moment. This mirrors a German tradition that recommends moving the beehives gently when the *Bienenvater* (beekeeper, literally 'bee father') dies. It is said that if the beehive is not moved, the bees will abscond or die.

The practice of knocking on the hive with keys or moving its location is not commonly regarded in Ireland. However, we are fond of leaving food from the wake or funeral beside the beehives, to welcome and include the bees in the proceedings. Spice cake, honey and mead were offered traditionally, and today this would most likely be a whiskey and a neatly cut sandwich.

The placement of black crepe or piece of material on the roof of each hive is a familiar ritual in Counties Cork, Limerick and Dublin and clearly demonstrates that a death has occurred in the family. The dark cloth is said to serve a dual function: it enables the bees to mourn and it restricts the bees should they rise to follow their keeper. Failure to adorn the hive with a dark cloth can also result in the bees' death, as the following 1961 account from Dublin states:

> *… san áit go mbeadh beacha, mara gcuirfí* 'crepe' *orthu (ar na cruiceóga) go bhfaigheadh na beacha go léir bás …*

> (… in the place where the bees are, if you didn't put a crepe on them (on the beehives) all the bees would die …)
>
> (National Folklore Collection)

Placing a piece of crepe, tied to a stick and fastened to the hive, is another common custom in the UK, as it gives the bees the opportunity to mourn. When Queen Elizabeth II died in 2022, the royal beekeeper, John Chapple, informed the bees in the palace apiary of the sad news. He placed black ribbons fashioned into bows on each beehive and shared the news that their mistress had died and that they would soon have a new master in King Charles III. Chapple, the official palace beekeeper for fifteen years, described how he knocked on the hives and requested that the bees stay where they were, with the promise that their new master would also be good to them. This reassurance is usual in folklore, where the bees are politely informed of one keeper's passing whilst being notified that they will soon receive a new master or mistress. In his 1880 book, *English Folk-lore*, the Rev. T.F. Thiselton-Dyer recorded the words to be spoken, as follows:

> Bees, bees awake!
> Your master is dead
> And another you must take.

In folklore, the origins of the ceremony of telling the bees is interwoven with the lore and legends describing bees' divine disposition. It is a practice that brings to life the belief that bees embody the souls of the dead. In pre-Christian times, birds, butterflies and bees were believed to be intermediaries between this world and the otherworld. Folktales describe the souls of the departed leaving the bodies of humans and animals in the form of the sacred bee. Therefore, by virtue of speaking with or telling the bees, we are, in fact, delivering the news to the messengers of the gods.

An alternative theory as to how this ritual originated has at its core the secularisation of beekeeping from the Church, owing to the Reformation and the suppression of monasteries in the 1500s. Monks no longer tended to large apiaries, and wax was less essential for the production of church candles. Sugar was also becoming less expensive, and so honey was not the only sweetener available. During this time, bees occupied a more significant role in family life, and thus the rite of telling the bees about family events reinforced their position of importance in the household.

Personally, I value superstition as it derives from long-held beliefs and values passed from one generation to the next. It also offers a layer of colour and playfulness to everyday life, and so I am an advocate of tying a ribbon to a tree on May Day, or *Bealtaine,* and look forward to receiving handsel coins – tokens of good luck – from my mother-in-law, Kathleen, at New Year.

With regard to telling the bees, I view the intimate act of confiding in the bees as the most meaningful aspect of this ritual. As children visiting Dad's bees in Wexford, my sisters and I would play while he worked with the bees in the corner of the field. He would be there for hours, tending to each hive as if tending to a baby in a cradle, feeding the bees, improving their levels of comfort, and leaving inconspicuously, as gently as he arrived. His calm and considered movements made it appear to me that he was working in slow motion, and now I understand what

> *It also offers a layer of colour and playfulness to everyday life, and so I am an advocate of tying a ribbon to a tree on May Day, or Bealtaine, and look forward to receiving handsel coins – tokens of good luck – from my mother-in-law, Kathleen, at New Year.*

a steady and meditative process it can be. The intimacy shared in this act of caring, with the bees and keeper alone in the corner of a field, provides the perfect setting to share some news, be it good or bad. Confiding in the bees holds that sacred assurance of secrecy. Your thoughts, your mood, your musings, your news: none would ever leave the sanctuary of the apiary.

Chapter Nine

RINGING A SWARM

… Do you notice how the note
has changed, he said, how it grows
lower and more certain? The bees
are about to swarm. They will gorge
themselves on honey, then be gone.
It is a beautiful sight and every
beekeeper's shame: the bees spilling
from the hive at noon; the Queen
in flight among them; the cacophony
of wings, the silence after.
I should meet them at the hive's
entrance as they leave, make my loud
lamentation with pot and spoon, try
coax the Queen back to her throne …

('The Silence After', Noel Duffy)

Bees spilling from the hive in a swarm is a sight to behold. It is majestic, and as visually and sonically intriguing as a murmuration of starlings. Each bee is given the space to fly, but they move in unison like a speckled cloud. When a swarm settles, a dense, spherical mass is formed, chocolate-brown in colour. They form a tight-knit cluster, with worker bees clinging to one another, and the queen embedded safely at its core.

Poet Noel Duffy in his poem 'The Silence After' mentions that there are some discernible moments that foretell an imminent swarm, such as specific movements and sounds emanating from within the hive. The swarming process is far from haphazard. It is intricately prepared for in advance, as the bees organise themselves fastidiously before flight. Scout bees determine the best location to orientate the voyagers, worker bees gorge themselves for long-term sustenance and, all the while, a new queen or queens prepare themselves, ensuring that the swarm that travels and the primary hive each has a leader in place, so that both colonies are sustained.

There are two main triggers or motivations driving the impulse to swarm: overcrowding and the birth of a new queen. A solution to overcrowding is for half the colony to leave. A new generation of bees hatching from the larvae adds pressure on space and honey resources, as well as increasing the temperature, and so the original generation of bees will be prompted to flee the hive with their queen. A division, or swarm, will be prompted by the birth of a new queen. A battle for supremacy can ensue when two queens find themselves in the hive simultaneously, and a solution is the departure of one of the queens, who brings with her a protective army of worker bees. A new queen can produce a series of unique sounds, known as 'piping', which are discernible to the human ear. Hearing this high-pitched tone is a good indicator of an impending swarm as it means there will be two queens in the one hive. My father describes this as a 'bleep, bleep' noise, and it marks the new queen's grand arrival. Other sounds can reverberate from the hive at swarming time also. A lower, more distinct hum is indicative of the worker bees stocking up on honey before embarking on their journey.

Folk stories describe the sounds and movements within a hive as critical indicators of an imminent swarm. An account from Cork in 1941 describes guttural sounds emanating from the bees. These were interpreted as messages being relayed from one bee to another, saying *'Chughat! Chughat! Chughat!'*, meaning 'To you! To you! To you!', and a response of *'Fág! Fág! Fág!'*, meaning 'Leave! Leave! Leave!' Dad recollects hearing his father, also a beekeeper, speaking of the discordant sound that heralds a swarm. He believed it to be the voice of the queen repeating 'Get out, get out, get out!'

A queen will ready herself before swarming. She will reduce her weight by releasing eggs, and will cut down on her food intake. Scout bees will investigate a suitable location to settle and will communicate the details to their sisters by the waggle and round dances. The scout bees will then lead the troops to their temporary resting place.

A conventional place for a swarm to settle is on the branch of a tree or the eaves of a house. There can be other less orthodox landing areas also. When Dad proactively collected swarms in the 1990s, being listed in the *Golden Pages* (the business telephone book) as a beekeeper, he received countless calls on hot summer days requesting the removal of swarms from households across Dublin and beyond. With several house calls every evening, I remember the long hours and hard work at this time, but it was well worth Dad's while, as his apiary expanded day by day.

When we arrived to collect a swarm, its location determined whether it would be an easy or challenging job. If it hung from a tree, the swarm was toppled with ease into a cardboard box, and it was my job to gently fold a white sheet around the bees and tuck them in. Locations that were more challenging were often the result of a swarm being more established in its new resting place. In this case, a scout bee might identify a sheltered spot between the indoors and outdoors, and nestle into a crevice in an attic, for example, where the swarm would go unnoticed for a while. This scenario made it more difficult to capture the swarm in one go, which in turn stirred the bees to anger. In such instances, one tactic is to isolate the queen, with the knowledge that the swarm will be encouraged to follow her, as this 1949 account from County Cork describes:

> Bees often settled down in quare places. I saw a swarm to get into the leg of an old trousers that was bleaching after being washed. I remember being in school wan day an' a swarm came in through the window an' started to settle down on a little girl's head. She was crazy out, but the master was used to bees, an' I think the swarm was his own too. He caught an' held her an' found the queen bee. He put her (the queen) out the window agin an' the rest o' the bees left the little girls head.
>
> (National Folklore Collection)

There are precautions a beekeeper can take to discourage swarming, although conditions can change quickly in high summer, making it more challenging to contain or deter. When all the cavities are filled with honey, brood and pollen, it leaves the queen without any comb area to lay her eggs. Bees will then start to build new queen cells, which appear like small thimbles facing downwards, signalling that cells are at capacity. A discerning beekeeper will detect this and work towards rehousing a portion of a hive, before the bees decide to manage matters themselves.

Folklore provides a wonderful selection of measures to safeguard against swarming. An ancient practice in Britain involved spraying the front of the hive with a mixture of warm water and wine, or smoking it with burning donkey dung so as to prevent swarming. Perhaps the potent smell urged the bees to remain indoors or, more likely, it was the calm-inducing effect of anbarnesa – the chemical produced from the smoke of burning female donkey's dung. In Germany, sourcing the afterbirth from a cow after her first calf and brushing this around the hive three times was said to mitigate swarming. The same result was achieved in a more domestic fashion in Palestine in ancient times, where a loaf of bread was rotated on the kitchen table three times. This ensured bees stayed put.

A tradition unique to the Irish is creating a special concoction on May Day or *Lá Bealtaine*. It involves blending equal measures of herbs and butter, and pounding them together into a thick paste. Applied to beehives, this mixture is said to prevent a swarm from leaving the hive. If it is too late and the swarm is already in full flight, throwing dust on top of the swarm will weigh the bees down, causing them to settle. Author Hilda Ransome, in her 1937 book *The Sacred Bee in Ancient Times and Folklore*, describes a lovely charm from Anglo-Saxon times to prevent a swarm fleeing into the woods.

Take some earth, throw it with thy right hand
under thy right foot and say …
Sit ye, Victory Women, sink to the earth,
Do not fly wildly to the woods,
Be ye as mindful of my good
As every man is of food and country.

The act of 'ringing' is an ancient method of intercepting a swarm in flight and coaxing the bees to settle. It involves banging objects together, such as pots and pans, and directing the loud racket in the face of the swarm. I am fond of the visual it conjures: of frustrated beekeepers or opportunistic onlookers following a swarm, clashing pots like cymbals and creating a wave of noise in a bid to make the rogue bees come to rest.

There are a variety of objects and materials that are effective for the purpose of ringing. Traditionally, instruments included old iron shovels, pots, tin cans, bells and spoons or sometimes the more musical option of playing a melodeon or beating a bodhrán. The following account, collected in County Cork in 1949, expertly describes the clattering and the commotion when a village is intent on ringing the bees. The rising of the swarm is called a 'pill-a-maloo' (from the Irish, '*pil a miliú*' meaning 'clamour'):

> She used know by the movements o' the bees a few days beforehand when they were going to swarm an' for fear they'd go they used be watched. That was the 'pill-a-maloo' when the swarm was up. Everywan in the house was out with something to make noise. Buckets, pans, hammered with sticks and irons, or old irons hammered together. The greater the noise, the better to bother the bees, an' make them settle down near home. 'Ringing the bees' they used to say. The Queen didn't like noise and couldn't lead the swarm very far.
>
> (National Folklore Collection)

It is interesting that the queen is described as disliking the loud racket and that it impacted on her ability to sustain her troops in flight. It is possible that the noise would drown out the queen's hum, preventing the bees from hearing her and following her lead. This provides one potential explanation as to why ringing is an effective measure against swarming. Finding it difficult to hear their leader, the bees become confused and disorientated, resulting in them settling down.

Virgil, writing in the first century BC, and Pliny the Elder, writing a century later, both attest to the curious method of banging pots as a swarm-gathering exercise. An alternative proposal was offered by Ovid (43 BC – AD 7), the playful Roman poet known for his mythological and legendary stories. Ovid maintained that bees love the sound of 'rough music' and that they choose to settle to appreciate the loud sounds! German tradition also depicts bees as music lovers. By contrast, however, the loud sounds entice the bees to swarm, rising up in a celebratory fashion, specifically in response to hearing church bells ring.

The practice of ringing bees has been documented in England for hundreds of years, but it is more commonly referred to as 'tanging the bees'. The *British Bee Journal* in 1971 described the effectiveness of tanging in the nineteenth century:

> When the swarm came out, he stood behind the hive rattling his poike and iron tray and the swarm did of their own accord at once fly down and take possession of that hive.

The 1969 edition of the *British Bee Journal* describes tanging the bees in the eighteenth century via the trusted method of beating pots:

> Sarah didd gett a pott ande beate itt harde wythe a spoon ande didd bange them till they didd bee quiet ande didd hange in one lumpe.

The origin and evolution of clashing pans to settle a swarm may have derived from laws developed in England in the ninth century. King Alfred, or Alfred the Great, King of Wessex (871–99) placed a high value on bees. During his reign, the fine for stealing bees was the same as the fine for the theft of gold or stud horses: 120 shillings.

King Alfred is said to be the first person to make candles with which the passage of time could be measured. This was the era when beeswax was the primary source for church candles. Alfred's bee laws decreed that when a swarm left a hive, the owner was obliged to announce this occurrence by ringing bells or banging metal to alert neighbours of a swarm in motion. This meant a swarm could be followed, identified, captured and returned to the rightful owner.

The act of ringing, therefore, may have begun as a public announcement that indicated a swarm of bees was on the move. With time, the reason for banging pots acquired other connotations and the act itself came to be understood as a way to settle a swarm, rather than a method of alerting people that swarming had occurred. This makes the tradition of ringing even more special in my eyes. The origin of the action and its final manifestation have different meanings and functions, as a result of the transference of a tradition by word of mouth over time.

Wonderfully, 'ringing the bees' is a common practice being carried out to this day. My aunt Marcella recalls locals in Ballindaggan, County Wexford, clapping their hands and making noise with the clear intention of confusing the bees and encouraging them to settle. During my research, I had the pleasure of speaking with John McCarthy, a beekeeper from County Louth. He described the act of 'ringing' to mean literally ringing bells to bring down a flying swarm. Ringing bells is how this tradition is celebrated and honoured at the annual beekeepers' harvest festival, which takes place in the Warwickshire town of Stoneleigh in the UK. A band of bell ringers comes together to perform for the bees.

An American harpist, Ann Heymann, who has researched Irish bee charms used to settle swarms, shared a collection of lovely associations she had unearthed about the honeybee and the *cláirseach* or Irish harp. Ann witnessed swarms being lured by the sounds of clanging brass, which is the traditional material used to make harp strings. She spoke of ringing the bees by playing her harp and how the bees respectfully settled nearby to fully absorb the vibration of the strings against the soundboard. Ann used a variety of instruments to serenade her bees, including a melodeon and a bodhrán. As musical instruments such as these have been used for centuries, it makes me wonder if playing to the bees is yet another way for us humans to connect with our little winged friends.

It is magical to witness this ancient beekeeping tradition in practice. Bees are accredited with a sensitivity that alerts them to the act of ringing, which incorporates music, language and movement. Whether it is in a bid to find and protect their queen, or to appreciate the loud sounds, it is yet another curious and beautiful tradition that is unique to bees alone.

Chapter Ten

BEES AS OMENS OF LUCK AND MISFORTUNE

The beloved bee is valued and respected through various lenses. Their work demonstrates a tenacious, industrious and harmonious community, for which they are held in high esteem in folklore. They are synonymous with what is wise, divine and moral, which serves to deepen the special connection that exists between bees and their keeper. Collectively, the impressive characteristics of bees has resulted in a culture of interpreting their movement and behaviour as indicators of good luck or portents of misfortune.

In Ó Donaill's *Foclóir Gaeilge–Béarla* (*Irish–English Dictionary*), published in 1977, a common fixture in many an Irish household in the 1980s, a '*cuasnóg*' (a nest of wild bees) is directly translated and defined as 'a lucky find'. The nuances implied by this understanding have infiltrated folklore, proverbs and riddles, where the arrival of a swarm of bees is deemed to be a lucky omen. Similarly, should a bee fly into a household, this is also perceived as a lucky sign. Whilst it is in the household, it is important to monitor the bee's behaviour. Should the bee fly in and out, good fortune will ensue, but should the bee die inside the house, this has negative connotations.

My aunt Marcella, born in 1928, is a strong believer in bees bringing good fortune to the household of their choosing. She maintains that bees will bring prosperity to homes that are peaceful, and whilst in this setting, the bees will flourish and produce top-quality honey. This was also a common belief in Northamptonshire in the UK and in France, where it is said that bees cannot survive in a quarrelsome household. If subjected to disagreeable surroundings, they will either desert their keeper or perish in the hive.

The arrival of a swarm is widely symbolic of good fortune. However, there is an interesting conflict that materialises within folk narrative regarding taking possession of a swarm, and the implications of this. As the occurrence of a swarm means it has come from a nearby hive, which is likely to belong to someone else, assuming ownership of this can pose a moral dilemma, as seen in this National Folklore Collection account from Cork in 1941: 'Some farmers say 'tis a lucky thing to have a swarm of bees come to you … Other farmers would never touch bees or have anything to do with them if they came to their land. They wouldn't claim them or anything … they say it is unlucky …'

A common thread emerges within folklore, describing misfortune coming to those who wrongfully claim a swarm. It goes against a moral code, and perhaps a beekeeping code, and the culprits are punished. A folklore collector working in the 1960s, John Delaney, noted that some of his interviewees had what he described as 'a superstitious fear of bees', believing them to be in some way 'bewitched'. Stories collected in Counties Roscommon, Longford, Kerry, Limerick, Cork and Fermanagh all attest to this, warning that a swarm will bring misfortune if claimed by the wrong owner.

When trying to make sense of this moral conflict, it is interesting to reflect on the Irish bee laws of the seventh century that existed as a subset of the Brehon Laws. Similar to the bee laws of Alfred the Great in England (871–899), the existence of the *Bechbretha*, or Bee Judgements, demonstrates the value of bees and honey to the Irish economy at this time. Interestingly, Brehon Laws were memorised and passed orally from one judge, or Brehon, to another, similar to the transmission of folklore. The *Bechbretha* worked hard to delineate between the rightful and wrongful ownership of swarms and determined the appropriate tax or fine to be paid to a neighbour should a swarm change hands. A law manuscript, currently housed in Trinity College Dublin, states that the finder of a stray swarm can claim it as their own property, but one ninth of the honey reaped from this swarm must be given to the finder's clan or church. It is possible that the arbitrary nature of these laws may have infiltrated and influenced folk belief and, at the very least, triggered a debate regarding rightful ownership and the moral implications of getting it wrong.

The specific landing point of a swarm, such as a tree branch, is regarded handsomely in folklore and can be put to good use. If a maiden was attending a dance, bringing a twig from such a branch on her person would help her identify a fitting partner. Presumably, the twig would orientate her in the right direction! In German tradition, the branch that hosts a swarm also delivers good results. Using this branch to direct your cattle to the mart, specifically on a Good Friday, would ensure a better price for the sale of your cows. Tapping the cows' back with the branch en route transferred a bit of good luck. Good Friday also holds significance in Cornish folk tradition, where it is regarded as the only appropriate day to move beehives.

Irish folk belief describes the consequences should someone interfere with beehives. An account from County Cork in 1949 shares how unlucky it is to interfere with or cause any injury to bees. A man suspected of smothering a hive to steal the honey is said to have been plagued with bad luck until the end of his days. A 1960 account from Cavan goes a step further, describing how a family member died shortly after the woman of the house took possession of a swarm. The two incidents are deemed intrinsically linked:

> This aul' woman went out about them, and she came over with a sheet and box and got them. She had a nice little hive for them. That was about June. There came home a son from England shortly after that and he wasn't hardly a month at home when he died. She had other troubles too; some of her stock died on her. So the bees didn't bring her any luck.

As the act of taking possession of a passing swarm is seen to attract adversity, folk tradition advises how best to acquire a hive of your own. Fundamentally, it is ill advised to sell or purchase bees with legal tender, as it invokes bad luck. In County Roscommon, it was said that bees should not be bought, but should come to you, perhaps by way of a gift. Bartering for bees, with items of equal value, is also deemed acceptable. In the UK, bartering bees was considered the best way to obtain your own hive, as money should never pass hands. In Sussex, specific commodities, namely gold or hay, are recommended as suitable barter for bees. The gold aptly complements the hue of honey, and such a transaction leads to a prosperous hive, where liquid gold is the payback:

When daisies fill the grass like snow
And blossoms white the trees
And to the bee-master I go
To buy a skep of bees.
I do not pay in brown money,
Or silver new or old.
Nay, that my bees may have good luck
I cross his hand with gold.
And now my bees they hurry forth
Till eve the dusk doth bring
And east, and west, and south, and north,
They go a' gathering.
The pollen and honey-food
They gather in four-fold
And all I paid the bee-master
They give me back in gold.

(*British Bee Journal*, 1970)

In Dad's home county of Wexford, there was an accepted notion that beekeepers starting out could only invest in a swarm with honest, hard-earned money. Similar to the older tradition that warns against bees being part of a transaction, the decorum adhered to around acquiring bees elevates their status above that of a mere commodity. Perhaps this mindset served to dissuade the fair-weather beekeepers, who might purchase a hive without fully understanding the weight of the investment and the responsibility of a keeper to care properly for their bees.

The traditions, folk memories and representation of bees in folklore often derive from this place of care. From the oral Brehon Laws to the transcribed *Bechbretha*, care was taken by the authorities to protect and safeguard bees and their produce, as they were an important facet of the economy. Care and camaraderie are at the core of the relationship between the bees and their patron saint, Gobnait. Within the folktales that marvel at and celebrate bees' intelligence and gentility, respect and care are shown to these creatures, which provide companionship, bring good fortune and deliver the comforts of food and light.

From my encounters with beekeepers all over Ireland, and from being by Dad's side for over forty years, it seems to me that the beekeeper is more of a caretaker or caregiver. It is a constant and special level of attention that positions bees as an integral facet of a beekeeping household. Yet, being independent and self-sufficient, bees will forever invoke in us that sense of wonder and curiosity. As caregivers, we are onlookers of these masters of ingenuity. It is our immense fortune to be involved in their work and in some way to facilitate the continuation of their reign, in nature, life and folklore.

EPILOGUE

Beekeeping has been an enriching and omnipresent feature of my life since childhood. My intention in these pages has been to weave together the different beekeeping strands that I have experienced over the years: as a beekeeper's daughter, as a folklore student, and today, as a carrier of old and new bee lore that deserves to be shared. Mostly, I have experienced beekeeping through observation. I have had the fortune to combine my childhood familiarity with beekeeping with my love of Irish folklore and to have carved out my own personal relationship with the bees in the process.

The climate crisis and mass extinction events pose new and unprecedented threats to the ancient relationship between humans and the bees. Milder winters and shifts in seasons are impacting the key ecosystem of pollination and honey production. The beekeeping calendar, which works in tandem with climate patterns, has altered to accommodate the unseasonably warm winters and extended periods of rainfall. The age-old proverbial beekeeper's saying, in use since the seventeenth century, has somewhat lost its meaning:

A swarm in May is worth a load of hay;
A swarm in June is worth a silver spoon;
But a swarm in July is not worth a fly.

Warmer temperatures and premature flowering are succeeding where Aristotle failed, by outsmarting the bees. Changes in climate are causing bees to breed and forage earlier, leaving them susceptible to unpredictable cold snaps in spring. Damaging pests such as the varroa mite, unique to honeybees, formerly remained dormant in colder months but now find honeycomb to be a hospitable breeding ground for longer periods of time. All the while, the honeybees' work as superior pollinators is threatened directly and indirectly. Nourishing food sources such as dandelions, weeds and wildflowers are being obliterated by pesticides and changes in land use, and the damaging effect of ingesting contaminated pollen is negatively impacting forager bees and hive productivity. The importance of addressing farming practices and the use of pesticides is underpinned by the knowledge that bees play an essential role in the maintenance of a balanced global ecosystem.

Thankfully, bees are again being recognised as highly effective pollinators, something known intuitively by our ancestors. The necessity to cultivate bees to ensure they can carry out their natural function is at a critical juncture. To tackle this, every individual, industry and government needs to play a part. There are encouraging signs, however, such as the ban on neonicotinoid pesticides in the EU, and a welcome upsurge in urban and rural beekeeping.

It has been heartwarming to witness Dad mentoring a growing number of budding beekeepers in recent years. Dad would not necessarily like to be viewed as a mentor, so much so that, while discussing this book, he has reiterated many times that his approach and my memory of it might not always be the best beekeeping solution. However, as with any trade, craft, art or skill, his is a deep-seated knowledge, an inherent understanding that comes from decades of focus and care being invested in one's passion. This is the stuff that cannot be learned on a course or read in a manual. It involves practice, error, learning, intuition, heartbreak, hard work and, potentially, reward.

I mention heartbreak because Dad experienced this in the late 1990s when his bees were infested by varroa. Before a control was developed to treat this parasite – which, ironically, was spread by beekeepers – the only remedy was to kill the bees alongside the infestation. The bees that Dad loved and cared for had to be killed by his own hand. This incident was akin to a death in the family. Dad contemplated giving up beekeeping altogether, as he could not cope with the thought of having to commit such a despairing act again.

He persisted, but this experience revealed to me the level of respect and loyalty he had for his bees, which he retains to this day. In truth, I am unsure whether Dad could ever hang up his beekeeping veil, but this occurrence meant he had to start from scratch: constructing hive by hive, erecting comb by comb and acquiring every healthy nuc along the way to build a strong apiary once again. Dad has lived through the changeable cycle of beekeeping many times throughout his life, meeting the encroachment of environmental challenges and threats. It is this lived experience and accumulated knowledge that he now passes onto the next generation of beekeepers.

In my experience, there is a wonderful kinship that exists between beekeepers. Dad is part of formal associations and informal groups of like-minded lovers of bees. With the knowledge of bees' vital importance to the ecosystem, combined with a certain glint of intrigue that bees ignite, Dad's beehives have been welcomed in various patches of land and gardens across Dublin, from the roof of his local GAA club, Naomh Olaf, to sheltered heritage sites and hospital grounds.

In recent years, it seems we are all becoming carers and keepers of the bees, playing a minor part in their magnificent existence. My hope is that these pages might afford an added insight into the folklore, customs, beliefs and traditions that these little creatures have inspired over centuries. The next time you indulge in honey, you might think of its divine origins, as well as its nutritional and delicious attributes, and count yourself lucky to be supping the food of the gods. When you light a beeswax candle, you might find yourself observing the flame and interpreting its flicker. Be sure to tell the bees when a loved one passes and seek solace in knowing that they too will mourn the loss. Should a swarm pass overhead, grab some pots and hammer them together to help the rightful owner retrieve their bees. And should you, like me, want a specific day on which to celebrate the bees, you might choose to do so with a nod to Saint Gobnait on 11 February, when the bees and their patroness are given the devotion they deserve.

BIBLIOGRAPHY

BOOKS

Barnes, Jonathan, *Aristotle,* Oxford University Press, Oxford, 1992.

Butler, Alban, *The Lives of Saints,* Burns and Oates, London, 1956.

Charlton, Jane & Newdick, Jane, *In Praise of Honey*, The Boyne Valley Honey Company, Drogheda, 1995.

Cowan, Cathal & Sexton, Regina, *Ireland's Traditional Foods: An Exploration of Irish Local and Typical Foods and Drinks*, An Teagasc, Dublin, 1997.

Crane, Eva, *The Book of Honey,* Oxford University Press, Oxford, 1980.

Crane, Eva, *The Archaeology of Beekeeping,* Gerald Duckworth & Co. Ltd, London, 1983.

Crane, Eva & Graham, Alexander John, *Bee Hives of the Ancient World,* International Bee Research Association, UK, 1985.

Digges, Joseph Garven, *The Practical Bee Guide*, Talbot Press Ltd, Dublin, 1950.

Duffy, Noel, *In the Library of Lost Objects,* Ward Wood Publishing, London, 1988.

Edwardes, Tickner, *The Lore of the Honey-bee*, Methuen & Co. Ltd, London, 1912.

Evans, E. Estyn, *Irish Folkways,* Routledge, USA, 1988.

Frazer, James, *The Golden Bough,* Wordsworth Editions Ltd, Hertfordshire, 1993.

Free, John B., *Bees and Mankind,* George Allen & Unwin, London, 1982.

Gmelch, Sharon (ed.), *Irish Life,* The O'Brien Press, Dublin, 1979.

Gojmerac, Walter, *Bees, Beekeeping, Honey and Pollination,* AVI Publishing Company, USA, 1980.

Gomme, George Laurence, *English Traditions and Foreign Customs,* Elliot Stock, London, 1885.

Gregory, Augusta, *Four Plays,* G.P. Putnam's Sons, London, 1968.

Inwards, Richard, *Weather Lore: A Collection of Proverbs, Sayings and Rules Concerning the Weather,* Elliot Stock, London, 1898.

Joyce, P.W., *A Social History of Ancient Ireland,* M.H. Gill & Son Ltd, 1920.

Kelly, Fergus, *Early Irish Farming: A Study Based Mainly on the Law-texts of the 7th and 8th Centuries AD,* Dublin Institute for Advanced Studies, Dublin, 1997.

Kelly, Fergus & Edwards, Charles (ed.), *Bechbretha: An Old Irish Law-tract on Bee-keeping,* Dublin Institute for Advanced Studies, 1983.

Knowles, Elizabeth, *The Oxford Dictionary of Phrase and Fable,* Oxford University Press, Oxford, 2005.

Lawson, John A., *Honeycraft in Theory and Practice,* Chapman & Hall Ltd, London, 1948.

Lyly, John, *Euphues: The Anatomy of Wit,* The Grenville Copy in the British Museum, London, 1581.

Lynch, Cornelius, *Gobnait: People and Places Associated with Saint Gobnait,* Con Lynch, Cork, 2023.

Lysaght, Patricia (ed.), *Food from Nature: Attitudes, Strategies and Culinary Practices,* Royal Gustavus Adolphus Academy for Swedish Folk Culture, Uppsala, 2000.

Maeterlinck, Maurice, *The Life of the Bee,* George Allen & Unwin Ltd, London, 1935.

Mahon, Bríd, *Land of Milk and Honey: The Story of Traditional Irish Food and Drink,* Poolbeg Press, Dublin, 1991.

Mollan, Charles (ed.), *Preprinted Papers on Bee Husbandry,* Royal Dublin Society, 1980.

Morse, Roger A., *Bees and Beekeeping,* Cornell University Press, London, 1975.

Murphy, Michael J., *Now You're Talking: Folk Tales from the North of Ireland,* Belfast, 1975.

Ó Catháin, Séamus, *The Festival of Brigit,* DBA Publications Ltd, Dublin, 1995.

Ó Dónaill, *Foclóir Gaeilge–Bearla,* Oifig an tSoláthair, Dublin, 1977.

O'Hanlon, John, *Lives of the Irish Saints,* James Duffy and Sons, Dublin, 1875.

Ó hÓgáin, Dáithí, *Myth, Legend & Romance, An Encyclopaedia of the Irish Folk Tradition,* Ryan Publishing Company Ltd, Staffordshire, 1991.

Ó Súilleabháin, Seán, *Irish Wake Amusements,* Mercier Press, Cork, 1969.

Ransome, Hilda, *The Sacred Bee in Ancient Times and Folklore,* Bee Books New & Old, Burrowbridge, 1986.

Robin, P. Ansell, *Animal Lore in English Literature,* John Murray, London, 1932.

Thiselton-Dyer, T.F., *English Folk-lore,* Hardwicke & Bogue, London, 1878.

Watson, James K., *Bee-Keeping in Ireland. A History.* The Glendale Press, Dublin, 1981.

White, Elaine C., *Super Formulas, Arts and Crafts: How to Make More Than 360 Useful Products That Contain Honey and Beeswax,* Valley Hills Press, USA, 1993.

Wright, Joseph (ed.) *The English Dialect Dictionary,* Henry Frowde Publishers, Oxford, 1905.

MANUSCRIPT COLLECTION, NATIONAL FOLKLORE COLLECTION (NFC), UCD

Main/Schools' Manuscripts Collection

NFCS 330:68 (Cork, 1937): *Verse describing Saint Gobnait*

NFC 1551:348 (Galway, 1959): *Beeswax recipe for skin ointment*

NFC 831:332 (Cavan, 1942): *Candles carrying a message*

NFC 306:482–6 (Cork, 1936): *The story of 'Harry Stattle'*

NFC 43:103 (Dublin, 1931): *Placing a crepe on a beehive*

NFC 808:24 (Cork, 1941): *Sounds made by bees before swarming*

NFC 1174:431 (Cork, 1949): *Swarms settling in unusual places*
NFC 1174:482 (Cork, 1949): *Ringing the bees*
NFC 789:311 (Cork, 1941): *Bees as omens of luck and misfortune*
NFC 1174:433 (Cork, 1949): *Punishment for interfering with a beehive*
NFC 1573:450 (Cavan, 1960): *Bees as omens of luck and misfortune*

Also referenced:
NFCS 15:176 (Roscommon, 1938); NFC 42: 148 (Cork, 1928); NFC 47:95 (Cork, 1933); NFC 54:92 (Wexford, 1935); NFCS 56:43 (Galway, 1938); NFC 789:311 (Cork, 1941); NFC 107:325 (Wexford, 1935); NFC 132:145 (Laois, 1935); NFC 272:493 (Kerry, 1936); NFC 303:92 (Cork, 1936); NFC 306:482–6 (Cork, 1936); NFC 327:280 (Cork, 1936); NFC 407:118 (Carlow, 1910); NFC 463:188 (Galway, 1938); NFC 482:284 (Carlow/Waterford, 1932); NFS 489:313 (Limerick, 1937); NFC 517:244 (Tipperary, 1938); NFC 556:236 (Cork, 1938); NFCS 591:264 (Clare, 1938); NFC 710:250 (Kerry, 1940); NFC 782:253–7 (Kerry, 1941); NFC 789:311 (Cork, 1941); NFC 831:332 (Cavan, 1942); NFC 864:466 (Cork, 1943); NFC 947:54 (Kerry, 1943) NFC 970:222–3 (Galway, 1944); NFC 1020:27–8 (Antrim, 1947); NFC 1129:137 (Cork, 1941); NFC 1139:270 (Cork, 1944); NFC 1172:427–8 (Cork, 1949); NFC 1176:256 (Cavan, 1949); NFC 1139:264–8 (Cork, 1944); NFC 1145:199 (Laois, 1942); NFC 1145:233 (Wexford, 1943); NFC 1163:50 (Longford, 1948); NFC 1172:431 (Cork, 1949); NFC 1215:426 (Tyrone, 1950); NFC 1231:469 (Mayo, 1952); NFC 1234:447 (Tipperary, 1952); NFC 1357:130 (Limerick, 1953); NFC 1386:48 (Antrim, 1954); NFC 1386:102 (Antrim, 1954); NFC 1499:304 (London, 1954) – A collector wrote a note in a manuscript when in London; NFC 1527:68–9 (Cork, 1959); NFC 1550:343 (Roscommon, 1959); NFC 1573:445 (Roscommon, 1960); NFC 1573:450 (Cavan, 1960); NFC 1575:116 (Roscommon, 1961); NFC 1594:527

(Cork, 1961); NFC 1594:83 (Cork, 1962); NFC 1623:153 (Louth, 1963); NFC 1691:133 (Louth, 1964); NFC 1754:17 (Sligo, 1968); NFC 1848:63 (Cavan, 1976); NFC 1849:63 (Cavan, 1975); NFC 1906:191 (Fermanagh, 1962); NFC 2105:124 (Limerick, 1978); NFC 2037:40 (Fermanagh, 1980); NFC 1386:102 (Antrim, 1954); NFC 1575:116–7 (Roscommon, 1961); NFC 1550:342 (Roscommon, 1959); Box 63, NFC Archive.

JOURNALS

British Bee Journal (BBJ), now managed by The British Beekeepers Association (BBKA):

BBJ 4233:309 (26.12.1970): *Rhyme for 'telling the bees'*
BBJ 4240:75 (03.04.1971): *Ringing the bees*
BBJ 4182:3 (11.01.1969): *Tanging the bees*
BBJ 4228:250 (17.10.1970): *Poem about honey*

Also referenced:

BBJ 4178:272 (16.11.1968); BBJ 4263:42–3 (19.02.1972); BBJ 4161:62 (23.03.1968); BBJ 4155:306 (30.01.77); BBJ 4183:122 (25.01.1969); BBJ 4263:42 (19.02.1972); BBJ 4263 (19.02.1972); BBJ 4223 (08.07.1970); BBJ 4196:176 (26.07.1969); BBJ 4263:43 (19.02.1972).

Bee Keeping Journal, Young Farmers' Club Booklet, No.2, The National Federation of Young Farmers' clubs for distribution by Evans Brothers Ltd, London, 1949.

Ériu/Volume 2, Meyer, K., and Strachan, J. (ed.): 'The priest and the bees', Gwynn, E.J., School of Irish Learning, Dublin, 1950.

MAGAZINES/PAMPHLETS

Ireland's Own Magazine, 'The Honey Bee in Lore and Legend' (09.10.1998)

Ireland's Own Magazine,'Saint Bees, Friend of the Poor' (12.08.1977)
Ireland's Own Magazine,'The Patroness of Beekeepers' (16.08.1941)
Pamphlet: 'Saint Gobnait of Ballyvourney', Eilís Uí Dháiligh (2001 & 2024)

ONLINE RESOURCES/EBOOKS

Aristotle, *Aristotle's History of Animals,* Translator: Cresswell, R., London, 1887: gutenberg.org/cache/epub/59058/pg59058-images.html

Aristotle, *Aristotle Generation of Animals,* Translator: Peck, A.L., William Heinemann Ltd, London, 1943: www.archive.org: https://rb.gy/29225f

Briggs, Helen, 'Prehistoric farmers were the first beekeepers', 11 November 2015: www.bbc.com/news/science-environment-34749846

Book of Judges, Chapter 14:1–20: www.bible.com: https://rb.gy/w4jsg1

Cassella, Carly, 'Bees witnessed using tools in nature for the first time … and it's really gross', 09 December 2020, www.sciencealert.com: https://rb.gy/9irgfr

Crocker, T. Crofton, *Fairy Legends and Traditions of the South of Ireland,* 2018: www.gutenberg.org: https://rb.gy/3c6zu6

Greshko, Michael, 'Oldest evidence of modern bees found in Argentina', National Geographic, 11 February 2020: www.nationalgeographic.com: https://rb.gy/b0d76f

Genise, J. et al., '100 Ma sweat bee nests: Early and rapid co-diversification of crown bees and flowering plants'. National Library of Medicine, 2020: www.ncbi.nlm.nih.gov/pmc/articles/PMC6989152/

Marx, Karl, *Capital: A Critique of Political Economy,* Translator: Moore, S., and Aveling, E., Moscow, 1995–1996: marxists.org/archive/marx/works/download/pdf/Capital-Volume-I.pdf

Newitz, Annallee, 'Bees are even smarter than we realized', 2017: www.arstechnica.com: https://shorturl.at/DRW5v

Owen, Aneurin (ed.), *Ancient Laws and Institutes of Wales*, Commissioners on the Public Records of the Kingdom, 1841: codecs.vanhamel.nl/Owen_1841

Pliny, the Elder, *The Natural History of Pliny,* Translators: Bostock, J., and Riley, Riley, H. T: www.gutenberg.org: https://shorturl.at/prnx5

Virgil, *The Georgics, 29 BC, Release date 2008: www.gutenberg.org: https://shorturl.at/Zm8Er*